GLOBAL HOLOCAUST

Global Holocaust

Copyright © 2016 Victor Ansor. All Rights Reserved.

No rights claimed for public domain material, all rights reserved. No parts of this publication may be reproduced, stored in any retrieval system, or transmitted in any form or by any means, electronic, mechanical, recording, or otherwise, without the prior written permission of the author. Violations may be subject to civil or criminal penalties.

Library of Congress Control Number:

ISBN: 978-1-63308-239-7 (paperback)
ISBN: 978-1-63308-240-3 (ebook)

Interior Design by R'tor John D. Maghuyop
Cover Illustration by Miša Jovanović

CHALFANT ECKERT
PUBLISHING

1028 S Bishop Avenue, Dept. 178
Rolla, MO 65401

Printed in the United States of America

GLOBAL HOLOCAUST

What You Should Know,
Expect and Be Prepared For

VICTOR ANSOR

CHALFANT ECKERT
PUBLISHING

TABLE OF CONTENTS

The Mandate 7

Dedication 9

Acknowledgment 11

Introduction 13

Chapter 1:   Economic Holocaust 19
Chapter 2:   Climate Change 29
Chapter 3:   Great Tribulation................... 35
Chapter 4:   Covenant of Exemption 43
Chapter 5:   The Great Outpouring
             of the Spirit 51
Chapter 6:   Great Harvest of Souls........... 61
Chapter 7:   Time of the Gentiles 73
Chapter 8:   Wealth Transfer 79
Chapter 9:   Prosperity of the Church 87
Chapter 10: Persecution of the Church 95
Chapter 11: Great Falling Away
             of Believers........................... 103
Chapter 12: The Nation of Israel
             and Middle East Crisis 115
Chapter 13: Era of False Prophets 121

Chapter 14: America in God's
                End Time Agenda 127
Chapter 15: Nigeria, a Nation
                to Watch 133
Chapter 16: Fulfillment of
                Biblical Prophecies 139
Chapter 17: Return of Power to Rome....145
Chapter 18: Finally the Rapture
                of the Church.....................149
Chapter 19: Antichrist Revealed 161
Chapter 20: The 144,000 Explained.......169

Epilogue 177

THE MANDATE

Unto me, who am less than the least of all saints, is this grace given, that I should preach among the Gentiles the unsearchable riches of Christ; And to make all men see what is the fellowship of the mystery, which from the beginning of the world hath been hid in God, who created all things by Jesus Christ: To the intent that now unto the principalities and powers in heavenly places might be known by the church the manifold wisdom of God, According to the eternal purpose which he purposed in Christ Jesus our Lord:

EPHESIANS 3:8-11

DEDICATION

To God Almighty the Revealer of secrets

and -

To the memory of my Mother Agatha,

who brought me to Jesus.

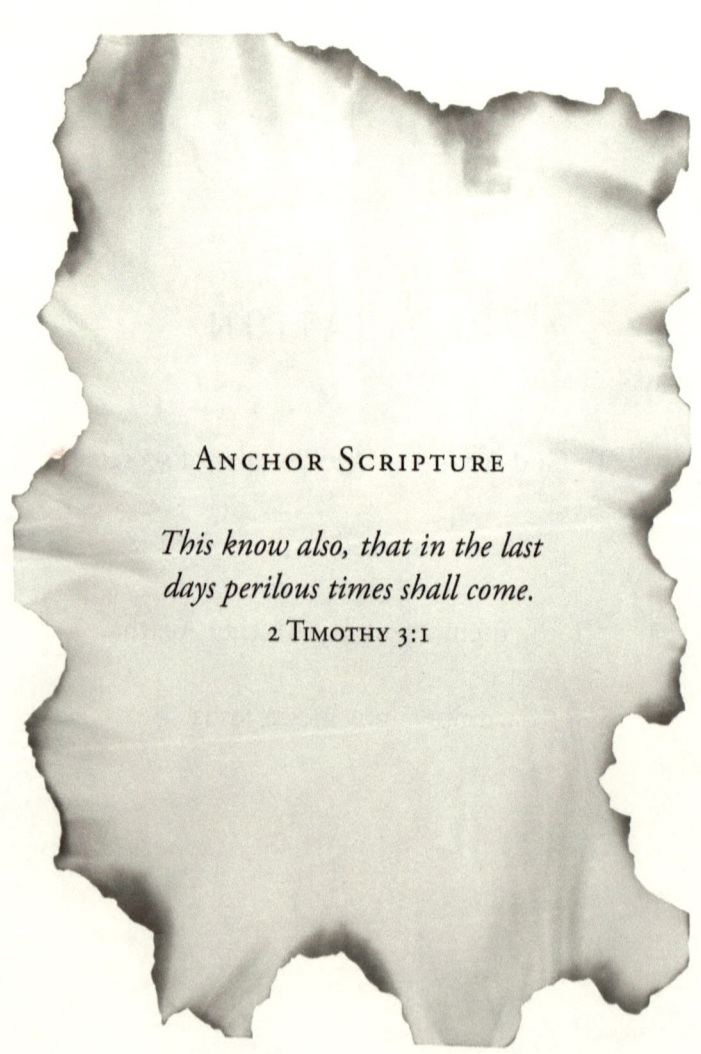

Anchor Scripture

This know also, that in the last days perilous times shall come.
2 Timothy 3:1

ACKNOWLEDGMENT

I acknowledge Almighty God, My Father in Heaven, for granting me life. Without Him, I could do nothing. I also acknowledge the person of the Holy Spirit who is my faithful companion. Wisdom and understanding I have none and without the help of the Holy Spirit, I would not be able to write this or any other book. I always sit back to read what I have written and every time I wonder how I did it. To me, that means that I am not the one who wrote it, instead it was the Holy Spirit who wrote through me.

This book and all my books have impacted my life and I hope they impact the lives of my readers. By the grace of God, I am just a pen of a ready writer, and I count it a great privilege to be in the service of God and to be an instrument He uses to propagate His Word.

I am thankful to my mother Mrs. Agatha, who has gone to be with the Lord. May her soul continue to rest in the Lord until we meet again when the trumpet sounds. She was instrumental to my being in Christ today. She took me to church and pointed me to Jesus.

Finally, I want to thank you, my readers. Without you, there would be no book. I also want to thank everyone who has encouraged me in one way or the other. May God bless you abundantly.

INTRODUCTION

We are living in a dangerous times, in the last hours of the last days of the end time. What is happening around us clearly defines the moment we are living in even to the most ignorant man. The Scripture calls it perilous times,

> *This know also, that in the last days perilous times shall come.*
> 2 TIMOTHY 3:1

It is not difficult to get away from the signs of the times. Television, Newspapers, the Internet, and modern technology devices remind us constantly of the gory events going on in the world. Everything is happening now, things we never imagined or never thought possible occur daily, giving us clues that something significant is about to happen. When Barack Obama, a black man, won the presidential election in the United States in 2008, the world witnessed the impossible happen. No one thought a black man would ever be elected as the most powerful leader in the free world. It was not until it happened that people started talking about prophecies that foretold that it would occur.

> *Declaring the end from the beginning, and from ancient times the things that are not yet done, saying, My counsel shall stand, and I will do all my pleasure:*
> ISAIAH 46:10

> *The counsel of the Lord standeth for ever, the thoughts of his heart to all generations.*
> PSALM 33:11

The happenings today are not just occurring because of human activities, but are carefully planned events. Things that were foretold thousands of years ago are being fulfilled with unimaginable speed. Therefore, we must wake up to the reality that the end is near. Even Hollywood is not left out as tons of movies depicting the end are being rolled out lately. This means that human beings are sensing the end of time, either revealed to them or by sheer instinct. Although Hollywood is making movies that show the world is ending, the devil is using those movies to make a mockery of God's agenda and cause men not to see anything serious about the end of the world. I recently saw a trailer for a movie about the end of the world and it said, "the world is ending, enjoy it while it lasts." You see, the devil has blinded the eyes of people so that they don't think about eternal consequences but instead enjoy the circumstances, even though the world is ending.

> *In whom the god of this world hath blinded the minds of them which believe not, lest the light of the glorious gospel of Christ, who is the image of God, should shine unto them.*
> 2 CORINTHIANS 4:4

The end of the world means that life will continue, although not on this earth. If this is true, what kind of life will that be? Man is a spirit and spirits don't die. Because a spirit doesn't die, what will happen after now? Will there be punishment for those who did wrong and a reward for those who did well? Is there a God who will judge the inhabitants of the world? "What really will happen after now?"

is the question everyone should ask themselves instead of just enjoying until the end comes.

The tide is turning, and mankind is playing his last and most important role since creation, and very soon the director of the movie set called "earth" will shout "cut," wrap up production, and the time for post-production will come.

Now is a time of chaos and mishaps for the world. The world has not seen anything yet as more terrible events are about to happen. But in the midst of all these happenings, those who walk with God will be gloriously distinguished, it will be a glorious moment for the church. These perilous times shall be times of prosperity for the children of God, while they will be a time of woes for the world. Many strong nations of the world will be humbled (as we have started to witness), and those nations will seek a solution from the children of God; in fact, during these times, God will clearly distinguish His people.

> *Then shall ye return, and discern
> between the righteous and the wicked,
> between him that serveth God
> and him that serveth him not.*
> MALACHI 3:18

You see, God will use this end time to set apart his children and glorify himself through them by what He will use them to do. What is about to happen in this end time is such that the world has never witnessed before. There will be terrible destruction on a mass scale that will make the hearts of men faint. In years past, we witnessed terrible events in some countries and the whole world rose up to help, but something is coming that will happen in all parts of the world so that help will not come from anywhere. Even our inventions and the genius of our elite scientists will all lead to the devastating end. Therefore, we all need to turn to the Almighty God through his son Jesus for help. When a nation sends God away from their system and embraces something else that is in opposition to God, that nation becomes an enemy of God. When you make God your enemy, you are bound to be destroyed. It is time we go to God in fasting and repentance just like the nation of Nineveh did when they heard that because of their sin, God would destroy them.

> *So the people of Nineveh believed God, and proclaimed a fast, and put on sackcloth, from the greatest of them even to the least of them.*
> JONAH 3:5

You cannot be too rich or too powerful to turn to God. No matter how rich or powerful a nation is, it can't stop a tsunami or hurricane. If a nation cannot stop these elements, then it must understand that there is a higher power which it must submit to. If the nations of the world will repent and acknowledge God, I believe God will stay his hand concerning what is about to happen. This is the book for the now, as it is timely. Therefore, make the most of what you read here for you never know what might happen next.

> *He that hath ears to hear, let him hear.*
> MATTHEW 11:15

CHAPTER 1

ECONOMIC HOLOCAUST

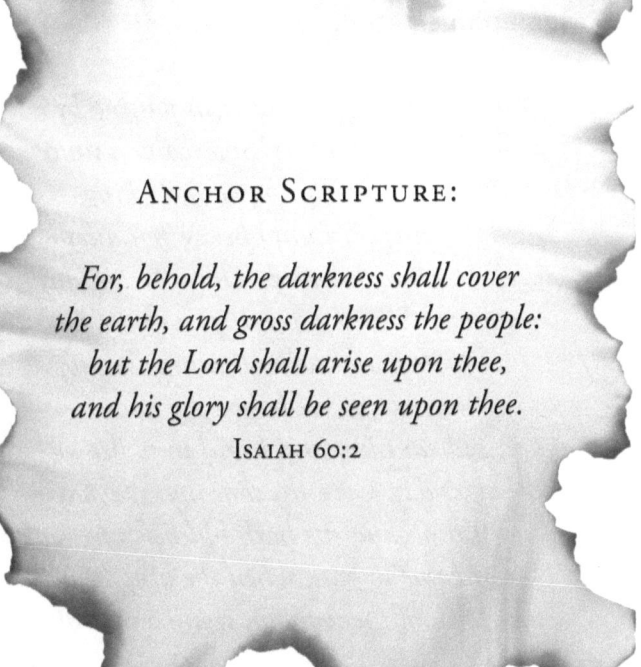

Anchor Scripture:

For, behold, the darkness shall cover the earth, and gross darkness the people: but the Lord shall arise upon thee, and his glory shall be seen upon thee.

Isaiah 60:2

THERE IS COMING AN ECONOMIC HOLOCAUST ON THE EARTH.

Economic holocaust is not new. There have been recorded droughts, famines, and terrible economic downturns throughout history, during which times man was thought to be on the brink of extinction. There were times when nations were helpless and could not profess solutions to the economic downturns that they faced. In 2 Kings 6:26, 28-30 we see what economic holocaust can bring upon a nation

> *And as the king of Israel was passing by upon the wall, there cried a woman unto him, saying, Help, my lord, O king. And the king said unto her, What aileth thee? And she answered, This woman said unto me, Give thy son, that we may eat him to day, and we will eat my son to morrow. So we boiled my son, and did eat him: and I said unto her on the next day, Give thy son, that we may eat him: and she hath hid her son. And it came to pass, when the king heard the words of the woman, that he rent his*

*clothes; and he passed by upon the wall,
and the people looked, and, behold,
he had sackcloth within upon his flesh.*
2 KINGS 6:26, 28-30

The economic holocaust experienced by the nation of Israel at that time was so severe and so terrible that parents began to eat their children. We have seen wars and famine in diverse places in the past that took away many lives. But what is about to happen in this time will be more severe than what the world experienced in the past. The time when many strong nations will be humbled is here. In Isaiah 60:2, the Scripture talks about gross darkness that will visit the earth:

*For, behold, the darkness shall cover the
earth, and gross darkness the people:
but the Lord shall arise upon thee,
and his glory shall be seen upon thee.*

The darkness that is mentioned in Isaiah 60:2 is not a literal darkness but an absence of a solution to the bogging issues of life. The time when the world will not know what to do will come. The absence of light is darkness and light means knowledge. There is coming a time when the world's economists and strategists will fail; they will certainly not know what to do. We saw a similarity of these impending events also in Genesis 41:56-57:

> *And the famine was over all the face of the earth: and Joseph opened all the storehouses, and sold unto the Egyptians; and the famine waxed sore in the land of Egypt. And all countries came into Egypt to Joseph for to buy corn; because that the famine was so sore in all lands.*

During that sore famine that lasted seven years, the world was at the mercy of Joseph. People could not handle the economic problems and could have become extinct if not for the divine wisdom of one man. Pharaoh relinquished power to someone who was previously a servant because God was with Joseph and revealed to him what to do to keep much people alive.

> *And Pharaoh said unto Joseph, Forasmuch as God hath shewed thee all this, there is none so discreet and*

> *wise as thou art: Thou shalt be over my house, and according unto thy word shall all my people be ruled: only in the throne will I be greater than thou.*
> GENESIS 41:39-40

God is going to teach this world a lesson economically; great nations will be humbled, and this will cause them to start seeking a solution from the church. A thick darkness is spreading over all the land and very soon it will be obvious that men of understanding and intellectual capacity have lost the ability to solve the world economic problems. There is coming a global drought for which countries of the world will soon face economic challenges and will not be able to provide food for their citizens. There will be famine that will destroy livestock, and the fish in the water will die. The food banks that are set up around the world for such a time will not be enough. But the paradox is that in the midst of all these happenings, there are people who will build, plant and succeed economically as happened in Genesis:

GLOBAL HOLOCAUST

And there was a famine in the land, beside the first famine that was in the days of Abraham. And Isaac went unto Abimelech king of the Philistines unto Gerar. And the Lord appeared unto him, and said, Go not down into Egypt; dwell in the land which I shall tell thee of: Then Isaac sowed in that land, and received in the same year an hundredfold: and the Lord blessed him.

GENESIS 26:1-2, 12

Therefore, it is not a new thing for the world to experience economic hardship while those who walk with God prosper in abundance. There had been diverse economic holocausts in the past but what is about to happen in our time is of a greater dimension because we are in the last days of the end of the world. There had been recent movies from the stables of Hollywood concerning the impending economic holocaust, but people only take it to be a figment of the imagination of the producer who only conceived such for entertainment purposes. I want to let you know they are not far from the truth because every movie produced has an essence of truth within the context, even though it may not be obvious to the casual viewer. We have seen rivers dried up in some places and fish washed to the shores. There are some places without drinking water while crops in other place refuse to grow because of some inexplicable factor. The truth is, all these happenings are gearing up to a mega-breakdown that will make the world experience the most severe economic downturn in history.

FINANCIAL HOLOCAUST

Money will soon fail. There was a time when money failed in the world, and that only shows that it is not a new thing that is about to happen, although what is coming is going to be more devastating and of higher proportion and impact than in the past.

> *And when money failed in the land of Egypt, and in the land of Canaan, all the Egyptians came unto Joseph, and said, Give us bread: for why should we die in thy presence? for the money faileth.*
> GENESIS 47:15

Many countries of the world today have a punitively high inflation rate; people take much to the market to buy little. Soon, people with all their money will not be able to buy anything because it will not have value, just like in the old days as recorded in the Bible. Money will soon fail; billions in banks will soon lose value, and the intellectuals and economists will not know where to turn.

In 1929, the stock market crashed which caused The Great Depression. This event ushered in global economic collapse, which was termed the deepest and longest-lasting economic downturn in the history of the western industrialized world at the time. In 1933, nearly half of the banks in the United States failed, and unemployment approached 15 million people. There was a 1987 stock market crash which was called the largest one-day market crash in history. The world woke up in January 2016 to experience another stock market crash which was occasioned by activities in China. We all know what happened in Greece, and soon other countries will follow. The oil prices are dwindling, and there is panic everywhere. If money failed in Egypt during

Pharaoh's time, surely it can fail in our time. As we have seen through history how money failed, the world should be prepared for what is about to happen because a terrible financial holocaust is about to happen.

CHAPTER 2

CLIMATE CHANGE

Anchor Scripture:

And the nations were angry, and thy wrath is come, and the time of the dead, that they should be judged, and that thou shouldest give reward unto thy servants the prophets, and to the saints, and them that fear thy name, small and great; and shouldest destroy them which destroy the earth.

Revelation 11:18

GLOBAL HOLOCAUST

CLIMATE CHANGE IS REAL.

Over the years, human activities have caused changes in the environment which have adversely affected life on earth. The anchor Scripture for this chapter says that God will destroy those who destroy the earth. If destruction awaits those who destroy the earth, then we must be wary of what we do on the earth. Lately, we have seen many changes in the environment which are the effect of climate change, wildfires, long period of drought, tropical storms, melting ice in the Arctic region and a rise in sea level, etc. In years past, we talked about the depletion of ozone layers, and to save the earth man must begin to plant trees especially in cities where there are no trees due to urbanization. The industrialized nations should be held responsible for climate change because of enormous emission of greenhouse gasses that have over the years adversely affected the earth. The above is a human explanation of climate change, but let's look at what the Scripture says about climate change.

> *The earth also is defiled under the inhabitants thereof; because they have transgressed the laws, changed the ordinance, broken the everlasting covenant. Therefore hath the curse devoured the earth, and they that dwell therein are desolate: therefore the inhabitants of the earth are burned, and few men left.*
> ISAIAH 24:5-6

Scripturally, the reason why the world is experiencing the so-called climate change is not really about human activities, but about sin against God. We have done terrible things that have made the earth operate under a curse and because of this everything is turned upside down. The earth has been defiled with innocent blood; there are ritual killings every day. Many have sacrificed their innocent children and wives on the altars of evil priests to obtain earthly wealth. Witchcraft is practiced in many places, and sorcery is common practice. God detests both practices. Men have neglected God and worshiped the devil. Because of this, even nature has turned against man, but we interpret it as climate change. The earth has been defiled and we no longer keep the laws of God. In fact, many nations of the world have removed God from their public lives and replaced Him with devil worship. A time for prayers has been turned into yoga practice and deep devilish meditation. They have changed the order of things, and the Bible says that because of this, the curse has devoured the earth. The Scripture also says that the earth shall become old, and we all know that when something gets old, it does not function the way it is supposed to.

> *Lift up your eyes to the heavens, and look upon the earth beneath: for the heavens shall vanish away like smoke, and the earth shall wax old like a garment, and they that dwell therein shall die in like manner: but my salvation shall be for ever, and my righteousness shall not be abolished.*
> ISAIAH 51:6

The earth is old and worn out according to the above Scripture, and it is a clear explanation of climate change. The Scripture says that because the earth will wax old, even those who live in it will be destroyed because of this change. The panic in the world today because of climate change is understandable because man knows that if nothing can be done to stop climate change, no human will survive. This theory explains the above Bible passage. Now that we know what God says about climate change, I believe the wisest thing to do is to surrender to God instead of trying to fix the earth because I believe it cannot be fixed. What is happening in the world today regarding climate is what was prophesied years back, and we know that the Word of God is true and has never failed. Let us wake up and surrender to God before the worst begins to happen because what has been purposed in the eternal counsel of God cannot change. Gathering at the United Nations will not save the earth, nor billions of dollars donated to the cause make a difference. It is time man turn back to his Maker for help.

CHAPTER 3

GREAT TRIBULATION

Anchor Scripture:

For then shall be great tribulation, such as was not since the beginning of the world to this time, no, nor ever shall be.

Matthew 24:21

GLOBAL HOLOCAUST

THE TIME FOR GREAT TRIBULATION IS HERE.

There is coming a great tribulation on the earth, the kind the world has never seen. We wake up every day to hear news of the outbreak of diseases, mass killings, terrorism, war, flooding, mass fire, hurricanes and tornadoes, etc. These happenings are just the beginning; the worst is coming. Jesus said that there will be great tribulation such that has never been witnessed on the earth from the beginning and after that such will never happen again. Recently we have witnessed ISIS executing Christians, and we condemn such barbaric acts. But I tell you the truth that these killings will continue. It is not about ISIS and Christians. ISIS' attacks will eventually come upon everyone. ISIS will bomb airports and train stations. As the civilized world beefs up their security to ward off attacks, they should be mindful of lone wolf attacks. Many individuals have ignorantly sold their souls to the devil and will carry out bombings in many locations around the world thereby causing great sufferings, pain, and anguish in a dimension never before witnessed. Nature will also work against man through natural disasters that will be beyond control. Oh, if man only knew what is about to happen!

> *For nation shall rise against nation,*
> *and kingdom against kingdom:*
> *and there shall be famines, and pestilences,*
> *and earthquakes, in divers places.*
> *All these are the beginning of sorrows.*
> MATTHEW 24:7-8

Every day of our lives, we hear of wars. There is no peace on the earth as tensions mount and tribal conflicts abound daily. If the terrible things happening around us are said to be the beginning of sorrow, then that means the worst is yet to come. Today, Israel and the rest of the world are uncomfortable with Iran becoming a nuclear power. Recently they tested a nuclear bomb and later sent a satellite into orbit, and no one could stop them. This event sent chills into the hearts of people around the world because the world knew what Iran was capable of doing. I want to tell you here that Iran cannot cause a nuclear war, neither will they launch any nuclear attack on Israel or United States. Although there will be no nuclear war now, the world should expect disaster from other sources both man-made and from nature.

Recently, we have witnessed passenger planes disappear that could not be found and the lives on board unaccounted for. Other aircraft have been fired down by speculative sources, while some crash in unexplainable manners. The way things are going shows that no one is safe, and none can escape the happenings. In the past, the world witnessed an outbreak of a deadly disease called HIV/AIDS and we thought that is the worst that could happen. But not long afterward, there was EBOLA, and now ZIKA caused by strange mosquitoes in South America. There was a strange disease discovered called LEGIONNAIRES caused by bacteria that grows in warm water and was found in cooling towers of buildings in New York. These are just a few of the newest diseases, as more terrible diseases are being found every day. But the truth is that more deadly diseases will emerge in many parts of the world. This is not to get anyone scared, but to enunciate the truth which you must know. I am not a prophet of doom as many will think, but am letting you know what to expect in the light of the Scripture. There will be terrible flooding and wildfires that will be out of control; great destruction is coming, but those who are on the Lord's side have nothing to fear because great is the Holy One In the midst of you (Isaiah 12:6).

News media are known for reporting negative happenings in the world. Seldom does a news article contain positive information. There is not a day that you switch on your television that you don't hear about kidnappings, murders, robberies, and house-fires with fatalities. There is a recent trend in New York City in which people are slashed on their way to or from work. Cars are hitting and killing people who are on the sidewalk. There are cars that leave the road and slam into buildings killing those inside. These types of events mean that unbelievable trauma has visited the earth, and no one is safe, even in their homes. The devil is bent on total destruction; that is why we are witnessing these happenings. The Great Tribulation is to usher in the Kingdom of Christ. Thus, these things must occur before the coming of the Messiah.

GLOBAL HOLOCAUST

*Immediately after the tribulation
of those days shall the sun be darkened,
and the moon shall not give her light,
and the stars shall fall from heaven,
and the powers of the heavens
shall be shaken:*
MATTHEW 24:29

There is no mention in the Scripture that the tribulation will end but will continue until Jesus comes. So what we see and hear in the news has come to stay and every day we will hear more dreaded things because it has been ordained to happen in our time. I recently watched in the news how a whole city was flooded, and you can imagine the untold hardship, pain, and sufferings that was brought upon the people who lived in that city. They virtually lost everything, and when the flood waters receded, they had to start all over again. I believe The Great Tribulation is to redirect the hearts of people back to God. Since we cannot stop The Great Tribulation, and the Bible confirms that it must happen, then we must return to God, and He will have mercy.

> *Let the wicked forsake his way,*
> *and the unrighteous man his thoughts:*
> *and let him return unto the Lord,*
> *and he will have mercy upon him; and to*
> *our God, for he will abundantly pardon.*
> ISAIAH 55:7

When we repent from our evil ways and return to God, that is when we will be saved from the evil days known as The Great Tribulation. The kingdom of darkness is on its final onslaught against this earth, and we will see this onslaught through the outbreak of new diseases that will destroy many lives. We will see more natural disasters and terrible happenings that will claim many lives and properties; but we can be divinely protected if we surrender to Jesus, and unless that happens, there is no guarantee of protection from what is coming.

CHAPTER 4

COVENANT OF EXEMPTION

ANCHOR SCRIPTURE:

But unto you that fear my name shall the Sun of righteousness arise with healing in his wings; and ye shall go forth, and grow up as calves of the stall.

MALACHI 4:2

> "YOU CANNOT PRAY OFF A PROPHETIC AGENDA, YOU CAN ONLY SEEK EXEMPTION."
> BISHOP DAVID OYEDEPO

There is a story of exemption in the Bible that authenticates how God can always exempt his people in time of holocaust. The reason why these people were exempted is that they were involved in the covenant and because of this, the holocaust could not have an effect on them.

> *And Moses stretched forth his hand toward heaven; and there was a thick darkness in all the land of Egypt three days: They saw not one another, neither rose any from his place for three days: but all the children of Israel had light in their dwellings.*
> EXODUS 10:22-23

There was a time when the darkness of holocaust covered the land of Egypt and for three days no one rose from where they were; everything was in the state of inertia. The land of Egypt was under the siege of holocaust and all activities ceased for three days. You can imagine if you woke up the next morning and the sun refused to shine and a thick darkness that could be felt covered the whole country so that not even light bulbs could shine, and no one could move from where they slept. Imagine the chaos and how many billions of dollars could be lost for those three days. Although the thick darkness covered the land of Egypt, the Bible says that the land of Goshen where the covenant people lived was light. The children of Israel lived in Egypt, but the city where they stayed had light while the remaining part of the city was covered in darkness. To be exempted from the wind of evil does not depend on where you live but on your standing with God. I hear about some people who run from a particular city and relocate to another because of the evil that happened where they lived before. There was a police officer who ran from the New York Police Department to another city because according to him, New York was not safe for his kind of job. But later, he died in the line of duty in that new state he thought was safe for him, and was brought back to New York for burial. I wept when I saw the news. Safety is only in God and not where you live.

GLOBAL HOLOCAUST

*Except the Lord build the house,
they labour in vain that build it:
except the Lord keep the city,
the watchman waketh but in vain.*
Psalm 127:1

Where you live does not matter, it is your standing with God and the covenant you walk in that matters. If you are a child of God and you operate under the covenant, let everyone around you die, you are exempted from it. The wind of evil does not respect location or zip code but the covenant. When you walk in the covenant, you cannot be affected by the winds of evil.

There is coming a global holocaust on the earth, but only those who walk in the covenant will be exempted from it. Those who will be stupid enough to obey God and walk in the dictate of his will can escape the scourge.

*Gather my saints together unto
me; those that have made a
covenant with me by sacrifice.*
Psalm 50:5

When you walk in the covenant with God, you are exempted from the holocaust. When we talk about the covenant of exemption, we are talking about those who have made a covenant with God to serve him with their resources. Note that the coming global holocaust will affect both Christians and non-Christians. A call to salvation is not a call to laziness but a call to responsibility. Therefore, don't think because you are a born-again Christian that the scourge of the holocaust will not affect you. An ignorant Christian can live poor on the earth and die and still make it into heaven. Therefore, you need to align yourself with the demands that will make you escape what is coming. The only guarantee of exemption from the holocaust is the covenant of tithing. Many do not know that the mystery of tithing is to secure our destiny as believers and to protect us from the evil of our days.

> *And I will rebuke the devourer for your sakes, and he shall not destroy the fruits of your ground; neither shall your vine cast her fruit before the time in the field, saith the Lord of hosts.*
> MALACHI 3:11

GLOBAL HOLOCAUST

The above Scripture is a true description of what holocaust looks like. There is coming a great destruction of lives and every hand work of man. The devil is the devourer, and he is destroying in this end time on a massive scale. To be exempted from this destruction, you must walk in the covenant so that God, who is the only one that can stop the devourer, could rebuke him on your behalf. No one can stand in the gap for you to be exempted but you must take personal responsibilities for your exemption. If you are not a tither, the devourer will have a field day in your life, and you are open to the holocaust.

There are many people from different religions who gather to pray against what is about to happen, but you certainly cannot pray off a prophetic agenda of God, you can only seek to be exempted from it. Obedience to the instructions of the Scripture is better than spending countless hours in prayers. If God says to bring the tithe so that the devourer can be rebuked on your behalf, it is senseless to fast and pray against the devourer because your prayers have no effect if you have disobeyed God in the first place by not tithing.

Just like in the land of Egypt when the whole nation was covered in darkness, but covenant people had light, the coming holocaust will distinguish between those who are the true children of God and those who are religious.

> *Then shall ye return, and discern*
> *between the righteous and the wicked,*
> *between him that serveth God*
> *and him that serveth him not.*
> MALACHI 3:18

There shall be a clear distinction between God's servants in the midst of the holocaust and those who are not his servants. The cloud of evil will pass over everyone who walks in the covenant so that the world will know that God is ever with those who obey him.

> *A thousand shall fall at thy side,*
> *and ten thousand at thy right hand;*
> *but it shall not come nigh thee.*
> PSALM 91:7

Even if everyone around you perish in the holocaust, as a child of God who walks in the covenant, you are exempted, no evil shall ever befall you. It is only with your eyes that you will see it happening to others. In the coming holocaust, the exemption right is not about how long you have been in the church, how big your title is, whether you speak in tongues. It is about your walk with God. Therefore, to be exempted, every child of God must obey kingdom demands of tithing so that they can be covered from the evil that is coming, for great is the holocaust.

> *And they shall be mine, saith the Lord of hosts, in that day when I make up my jewels; and I will spare them, as a man spareth his own son that serveth him.*
> MALACHI 3:17

To those who fear God and are willing to do things according to his dictates, God promised that they shall live well, and the holocaust will not have any effect on them. This is why you don't experience any symptoms of new diseases, and the road you walk on is the same road that claimed other lives. God says that in the midst of the holocaust, his own children will prosper, and they shall not have any reason to fear.

CHAPTER 5

THE GREAT OUTPOURING OF THE SPIRIT

ANCHOR SCRIPTURE:

And it shall come to pass in the last days, saith God, I will pour out of my Spirit upon all flesh: and your sons and your daughters shall prophesy, and your young men shall see visions, and your old men shall dream dreams: And on my servants and on my handmaidens I will pour out in those days of my Spirit; and they shall prophesy:

ACTS 2:17-18

GLOBAL HOLOCAUST

REVIVAL IS SWEEPING THROUGH THE EARTH IN THIS END TIME.

The Holy Spirit of God is in his last phase of operation on the earth. This world is going to experience a massive operation of the spirit in this end time, in a dimension never before witnessed. It is the era of the rise of Kingdom giants on the earth. Children of God will begin to operate in divine frequencies because of the outpouring of the Spirit. Something is about to happen in the body of Christ and the whole world that has never been witnessed before. Children of God are going to take over the affairs of this world because of the great outpouring of the Spirit of God on the earth. Oh, I can see with the eyes of my spirit man! Great evangelists will operate under great anointing, healing the sick and performing great miracles as never recorded in the history of the revival of the church. Pastors who will not take advantage of the flock but will nurture them with the integrity of their hearts and the skillfulness of their hands, thereby preparing a people ready to receive their Messiah.

There is coming a great revival in this end time that will be greater than the Upper Room and the Azusa Street Revival. There will be a rise of evangelists and revivalists, greater than Kathryn Kuhlman, Oral Roberts, Kenneth Hagin, Smith Wigslesworth, John G. Lake, Bishop David Oyedepo, Pastor E. Adeboye, Benny Hinn, Arch Bishop Benson Idahosa, etc. The great outpouring of the Spirit of God in this end time will raise men who will dominate this earth and usher in the Kingdom of God.

A great revival is sweeping through the earth, and those we thought would never make heaven are the ones who will become Kingdom giants in this end time.

So the last shall be first, and the first last: for many be called, but few chosen.
MATTHEW 20:16

Those people the church leaders condemned and rejected are the people who will serve God with great passion in this end time. Those who had been outcast and seen as not spiritual enough for God to use are the ones that will be full of the Spirit and will do great exploits in the Kingdom.

The outpouring of the Spirit will make the children of God dominate every area of endeavor. They shall take over industry; they shall enter politics and dominate and rule. Therefore, it is time for the children of God who were afraid of joining politics to enter without fear because, by the outpouring of the Spirit, every child of God shall dominate in their fields. When the Spirit of God came upon David, he was needed in the palace. By reason of the outpouring of the Spirit of wisdom upon Joseph, the king sent for him. Likewise, because of the outpouring of the Spirit of God upon his people in this end time, presidents will seek God's children to tap from their wisdom to solve the problems of the nations.

By the outpouring of the Spirit, this earth is going to be visited by divine wisdom, the kind the world has never seen. Children of God will begin to operate with higher wisdom than Daniel, Joseph, and Solomon. Wisdom will make people seek after them. As a child of God, wherever you are, begin to prepare yourself because you are taking over. Divine wisdom and insight are visiting the body of Christ because of the outpouring of the Spirit.

> *But Peter, standing up with the eleven, lifted up his voice, and said unto them, Ye men of Judaea, and all ye that dwell at Jerusalem, be this known unto you, and hearken to my words:*
> ACTS 2:14

Because of the outpouring of the Spirit upon Peter, a very shy and reluctant man who was hiding from the authorities came out and spoke the Word of God with boldness. The outpouring of the Spirit in this end time will raise men that were reluctant and shy like Peter to go into the highways and hedges of the earth and preach the Word of God without fear.

> *And it shall come to pass in the last days, saith God, I will pour out of my Spirit upon all flesh: and your sons and your daughters shall prophesy, and your young men shall see visions, and your old men shall dream dreams: And on my servants and on my handmaidens*

GLOBAL HOLOCAUST

*I will pour out in those days of my
Spirit; and they shall prophesy:*
ACTS 2:17-18

The outpouring of the Spirit of God in this end time is for every child of God and not only for pastors and church leaders. Those that were in the background and counted as nothing will, because of the Spirit, begin to function in capacities never thought possible. We shall begin to see notable miracles in every church service because the Spirit of God will come mightily upon his people. Church services will not be like before where nothing happens and day in day out people come in with needs and return with the same need. Church services will no longer be a social gathering but a true spiritual gathering where the presence of God will be visible. Because of the outpouring of the Spirit, there shall be diverse healing and deliverance in every church service. The lame will enter into the church and return walking with dignity. Anyone with diseases will receive instant healing, and the name of Jesus will be glorified. Members of the church will begin to do miracles wherever they are because of the Spirit of God.

> *And John answered and said,*
> *Master, we saw one casting out devils*
> *in thy name; and we forbad him,*
> *because he followeth not with us.*
> Luke 9:49

The outpouring of the Spirit is to restore the dignity of God's people; that is why the Scripture says that when the spirit comes; there shall be restoration of the years that the enemy took away through sickness, diseases, and calamities. There shall be total restoration of wasted years and the name of Jesus will be glorified.

> *And I will restore to you the years that the*
> *locust hath eaten, the cankerworm,*
> *and the caterpiller, and the palmerworm,*
> *my great army which I sent among you.*
> *And ye shall eat in plenty, and be satisfied,*
> *and praise the name of the Lord your God,*
> *that hath dealt wondrously with you:*
> *and my people shall never be ashamed.*
> Joel 2:25-26

The outpouring of the Spirit of God in this end time will cause a great awakening and revival on the earth so that where the gospel of Christ was impossible to be preached, there will be a great number of people turning to Christ. The revival will also affect other religions as many will abandon their religion and follow Christ. Cities that were notorious in worshiping other gods will turn to Jesus and declare Christianity as their official religion. When we see this happening, let no man take the credit because it is an agenda of heaven and not the effort of any evangelist or missionary.

I recently watched online a group of children who gathered to pray, and they were full of the Spirit and began to speak in tongues for hours, I mean little children praying in the Spirit. I could feel the power of God moving in their midst. This is called revival, and this revival is visiting the earth greatly, and many people will surrender to Jesus thereby making the gospel enter everywhere for a witness before the end comes.

> *And this gospel of the kingdom*
> *shall be preached in all the world*
> *for a witness unto all nations;*
> *and then shall the end come.*
> MATTHEW 24:14

It is this revival that will make people carry the gospel to where it was impossible before. Missionaries will no longer fear being caught by wicked rulers but will enter impossible countries and preach the everlasting gospel to the lost. They will be amazed at how many will receive the gospel as if they had been waiting all their lives for it. Let the church begin to prepare to send missionaries to areas they couldn't enter before because the time when the heart of men is prepared to receive Jesus is now.

CHAPTER 6

GREAT HARVEST OF SOULS

ANCHOR SCRIPTURE:

*And it shall come to pass
in the last days, that the mountain
of the Lord's house shall be established
in the top of the mountains,
and shall be exalted above the hills;
and all nations shall flow unto it.*

ISAIAH 2:2

GLOBAL HOLOCAUST

THERE SHALL BE A GREAT INFLUX OF SOULS INTO THE BODY OF CHRIST IN THIS LAST DAYS.

The after effect of the outpouring of the Spirit of God upon the earth shall be the influx of a multitude of souls into the church. The church will expand and increase in this end time, and many churches will not even have enough space to accommodate the multitudes that are coming. The time has come when a whole city, notorious for paganism, will be converted to Jesus, and streets will be empty in some cities during church service. The time has come when the hearts of men will turn to God, and they shall seek him with all their heart.

That they should seek the Lord, if haply they might feel after him, and find him, though he be not far from every one of us:
ACTS 17:27

I was in the church very early one day and preparing it for the midweek service when a woman walked in and asked for the time of service, but then she made a remarkable statement that struck something in me. She said, "I am looking for where I can start worshiping God."

And it shall come to pass in the last days, that the mountain of the Lord's house shall be established in the top of the mountains, and shall be exalted above the hills; and all nations shall flow unto it.
ISAIAH 2:2

There is coming a great harvest of souls into the church in these last days. The Bible says that in the last days, nations shall flow into the church and if the Word of God says that nations shall flow, then of a truth we shall witness an influx of nations into the church. The church shall be exalted above every other and shall be established at the very top so that everyone will desire to be a part of it. The time has come when the unsaved souls will walk into the church on their own without anyone preaching to them and surrender their lives to Jesus. God is calling for souls of men to be delivered, and many churches are heeding this call of the Spirit by engaging vigorously in evangelism. The world is about to end, and the

Spirit is crying out for souls saying, "Just one soul." You never know if your engagement in the soul drive will save someone who was on the way to hell.

By the power of the Holy Spirit, there shall be a great deliverance of souls of the multitude from destruction. Those we never thought would make heaven are the ones we will see coming to surrender to Jesus. Prostitutes, gangsters, atheists, drug dealers, pimps, and devil worshipers, etc. Those we disdain and think cannot be saved are the ones who will become great in the Kingdom. Those we see as bad and outcasts are the ones coming in to populate the Kingdom of God. The criminals are all going to convert to Jesus, and the house of God will be full.

*And the lord said unto the servant,
Go out into the highways and
hedges, and compel them to come
in, that my house may be filled.*
LUKE 14:23

It is time we go out into every corner of the city where we are and compel people to come to church. Let the leaders of the church begin to prepare themselves to handle the influx of multitude of souls because they are coming, not because they like a particular church, but because it is their time to come. As you engage in evangelism, don't despise anyone neither be afraid to talk to anyone because the time for them to come to Jesus is now.

Thus saith the Lord of hosts;
In those days it shall come to pass,
that ten men shall take hold out of all
languages of the nations, even shall take
hold of the skirt of him that is a Jew,
saying, We will go with you:
for we have heard that God is with you.
ZACHARIAH 8:23

The time is coming and now is when people will walk up to you and tell you to take them to church because of what they have seen in your life. Therefore, it is time born-again Christians rightly position themselves so that the glory of God will manifest in their lives so that nonbelievers desire to follow them to church. The time is coming when you will not need to do vigorous evangelism because your life will attract people to God and no longer your words. God's church will soon become a city without walls by reason of the influx of multitudes into the church. It will surprise you to know that even presidents of nations and captains of industries and the wealthy men of substance will run to the church because of what they see happening there. Great men will begin to seek God, and those who rejected God before will come bowing unto Jesus because the kingdom of this world shall become the Kingdom of our Lord and of His Christ. The Bible says that all nations shall flow into the church, and we see that happening already. To be sure they are in the right place of worship, we must bring them into where we are to see them genuinely established in the faith. We must not allow souls who are running to Jesus to fall into wrong hands that will destroy them instead of save them. The great harvest of souls in this end time is not to populate the church but to populate the Kingdom of God. Churches should not see the influx of multitudes as an increase in their membership but the saving of the lost from the grip of the devil.

VICTOR ANSOR

In the multitude of people is the king's honour: but in the want of people is the destruction of the prince.
Proverb 14:28

The king must come and meet his church with the great multitudes who will welcome him. God's church must be populated, and this is why the winds of the Spirit will blow the harvest fields of souls, and many will be harvested into the church in numbers unimaginable. God has released his reaper angels into the harvest field and all we have to do as the church is to move in and collect them into the fold. It will amaze you in this end time as how easy you will find people responding to the call of salvation because they are ripe for salvation.

Then saith he unto his disciples, The harvest truly is plenteous, but the labourers are few;Pray ye therefore the Lord of the harvest, that he will send forth labourers into his harvest.
Matthew 9:37-38

The harvest field of souls in this end time is plentiful, but those who will work in this harvest season are few. Therefore, we must engage in prayers for God to touch the hearts of men so that they can make the most of this season by engaging in the harvest. God needs men who will work for him this season. Therefore, we must make ourselves available to him. The greatest task that God has for the end time church is to reach out to the lost souls, this is the mind of God. The Scripture says that it is not his will that souls should perish but that they come to repentance.

> *The Lord is not slack concerning his promise, as some men count slackness; but is longsuffering to us-ward, not willing that any should perish, but that all should come to repentance.*
> 2 PETER 3:9

God does not want anyone to go to hell. Therefore, He is crying out through his Spirit to the church to reach out to them so they can be saved. It is a great harvest, and the church must take this task as a priority. The engagement in the soul drive in this end time should not be seen as a program to increase church membership but of saving the lost. Thus, we must engage in it with all our hearts to maximize the blessedness of the season. Your most glorious moment in heaven will be to see someone you invited to church who made it to heaven. It will be very wonderful for every child of God to see the souls they brought to church in white robes greeting Jesus. They will know it is because of their efforts for the Kingdom that those souls are in heaven.

As Christians, we must understand that people of other religions are hungry for true spiritual connection. They are genuine people who are genuinely desiring to connect with God. The Muslims, Buddhists, Hindus, Baha'is, pagans, and others long for the supernatural. The reason why they worship who or what they worship is not their fault, but what they were born into, made to believe, or introduced to at a point in time when they knew nothing better. If they had been introduced to Christianity at the point when they had contact with the other religion, they would have accepted Jesus the way they accept their present religion. We also must understand that God loves everyone irrespective of what they worship, and that Jesus did not die for just Christians, He died for everyone.

> *For God so loved the world,*
> *that he gave his only begotten Son,*
> *that whosoever believeth in him should*
> *not perish, but have everlasting life.*
> JOHN 3:16

The love of God that made him send his son to die is for the whole world and not a particular set of people. Therefore, in reaching out to the lost souls, we should be mindful of the messages we preach. Many sermons, both in the pulpit and in the street, have pushed people away from Christ instead of bringing them to Him. Some Christians are fond of preaching a message of condemnation instead of the love of God. Jesus did not come to condemn anyone but to show love and bring everyone to God.

> *For God sent not his Son into the world*
> *to condemn the world; but that the*
> *world through him might be saved.*
> JOHN 3:17

We must fine tune our message in this end time to pull people to Jesus. I have passed many bus and train stations and heard people preaching a message of condemnation. You don't go around shouting and telling people that they will die if they don't stop doing this or that. If you go about preaching that way, no one will listen to you, and few will respond positively. The devil has tormented and afflicted many souls. Whatever they do as sin, many times are the things they don't want to do. To draw them to Jesus, you must show them the love Jesus has for them and give them a reason to come to Him. When they come to Jesus, the Holy Spirit will convict them of sin, and they will surrender their lives to Jesus.

And when he is come,
he will reprove the world of sin,
and of righteousness, and of judgment:
JOHN 16:8

Finally, as the church has begun to experience an influx of multitudes, and those we never believed would come to the church are now surrendering to Jesus, let the church begin to show love and care and reach out to everyone irrespective of religion, race, or color. Let every child of God love everyone around them, whether they are Muslims, Hindus, Buddhists, pagans or atheists. These lost souls will begin to flock to the church, surrender to Jesus, and be rooted and established in the faith and make heaven. This is the agenda of heaven for the end time.

CHAPTER 7

TIME OF THE GENTILES

Anchor Scripture:

And they shall fall by the edge of the sword, and shall be led away captive into all nations: and Jerusalem shall be trodden down of the Gentiles, until the times of the Gentiles be fulfilled.

Luke 21:24

THE TIME WE ARE LIVING IN IS CALLED THE TIME OF THE GENTILE.

A Gentile is one who is not a Jew. This is the time of the Gentiles and very soon the times of the Gentiles will be over. The reason why the Jews are suffering great persecution and even threat to their homeland by it neighbors is that, by divine order, it is allowed. Jews in Jerusalem particularly suffer because Muslims built their mosque called "the Dome of the Rock" on the Temple Mount, right where the Jewish Temple was destroyed by the Romans in 70 A.D. It is also the spot that three religions (Christianity, Judaism, and Islam) believe to be Mount Moriah, the site where Abraham went to sacrifice his son, although Muslims believe it was son Ismael instead of Isaac. It is the very spot where the angel who was slaughtering the men in Israel stood, and King David bought the spot from Araunah and offered sacrifice unto God.

And when the angel stretched out his hand upon Jerusalem to destroy it, the Lord repented him of the evil, and said to the angel that destroyed the

*people, It is enough: stay now thine hand.
And the angel of the Lord was by the
threshingplace of Araunah the Jebusite.
And the king said unto Araunah,
Nay; but I will surely buy it of thee at a
price: neither will I offer burnt offerings
unto the Lord my God of that which doth
cost me nothing. So David bought the
threshingfloor and the oxen for fifty
shekels of silver. And David built there
an altar unto the Lord, and offered burnt
offerings and peace offerings.
So the Lord was intreated for the land,
and the plague was stayed from Israel.*
2 SAMUEL 24:16, 24-25

That is the very spot where King Solomon built a magnificent temple unto the Lord that caused many kings to travel far and wide, including the Queen of Sheba, to see the wonders of the temple. The reason why God allows the Muslim to desecrate the temple site and built their mosque there is because it is the times of the Gentiles.

Jesus said that Jerusalem shall be trampled underfoot, and we have seen that fulfilled before our very eyes. Jerusalem is the most contested piece of land on the earth dating back thousands of years. Israel is the most hated nation on the earth, and many want to destroy it. But I tell you the truth and I lie not, by the light of the Scriptures, no nation under the sun shall be able to destroy Israel. No matter how hard they try, they cannot succeed. I know the concern of Israel's prime minister going around to muster support for Israel and seeking resolutions in the United Nations to stop Iran and others from acquiring nuclear weapons. There is no need for fear because their weapons are not for the destruction of Israel, but a piling up for the total destruction of the earth at the very end.

> *But the day of the Lord will come as a thief in the night; in the which the heavens shall pass away with a great noise, and the elements shall melt with fervent heat, the earth also and the works that are therein shall be burned up.*
> 2 PETER 3:10

Over the years, we have seen Israel suffer greatly in the hands of the Gentiles. Many kings in the ancient times pillaged their land, killed millions of them, and took them from their land into strange lands where they lived as slaves for many years. The times of the Gentiles started when King Nebuchadnezzar carried the Jews from their land to Babylon and since then, they had not settled in their country until their final return in 1948. During the Holocaust, Hitler tried to annihilate the Jews completely and although he didn't succeed, it is estimated that six million Jewish people were killed. The reason Israel suffers is that the Gentiles have been given time to do whatever they like before they are judged.

> *And they shall fall by the edge*
> *of the sword, and shall be led away*
> *captive into all nations: and Jerusalem*
> *shall be trodden down of the Gentiles,*
> *until the times of the Gentiles be fulfilled.*
> LUKE 21:24

GLOBAL HOLOCAUST

The time of the Gentiles will soon be over, and God will establish the Jews forever in a kingdom where they will neither be harassed, threatened, or moved. The Jews will rule over all the earth and Jesus who is a Jew will be the King of Kings and Jerusalem shall be the center of authority on the earth.

CHAPTER 8

WEALTH TRANSFER

Anchor Scripture:

And the children of Israel did according to the word of Moses; and they borrowed of the Egyptians jewels of silver, and jewels of gold, and raiment: And the Lord gave the people favour in the sight of the Egyptians, so that they lent unto them such things as they required. And they spoiled the Egyptians.

Exodus 12:35-36

GLOBAL HOLOCAUST

IT IS TIME FOR WEALTH TRANSFER.

There was a time in history when the wealth of a nation was transferred to a particular set of people who were the children of God. The nation of Egypt was the wealthiest nation at the time, but they woke up one day, and all their wealth was transferred to people who were once their slaves. To compensate the children of Israel for their service of four hundred and thirty years of slave labor to Egypt, God turned Egypt's wealth over into the hands of the children of Israel and the Egyptians could not do anything about it.

There is coming a transference of wealth in this end time from the hand of the children of the world into the hands of the children of God. The wealth of nations will enter the hands of God's children who had been walking before God in true service. Therefore, it is time for the children of God to buy stocks and invest in real estate. God's children should become involved in politics and engage in international business because it is time for wealth transfer. In this time, any small investment of a child of God will turn into global investment because we are right at the very moment in God's end-time plan for wealth. When the world begins to sell, children of God should not be afraid to buy. As a child of God, when people offer you properties that seem too good to be true, don't be afraid to buy because it is your time. That is why it is happening. If you have been serving God faithfully and for a while and it seemed you haven't gotten anything from it and you are discouraged, I tell you not to relent because the time for your reward has come. Men who look like nothing today will take over industries and positions they never dreamed of. Small business will soon turn global. There will be quantum leaps in every endeavor of believers that will make the world wonder.

> *A little one shall become a thousand,*
> *and a small one a strong nation:*
> *I the Lord will hasten it in his time.*
> ISAIAH 60:22

Those who are seemingly little now in the body of Christ will soon become like a thousand, and the smallest child of God will soon become a global phenomenon. Therefore, do not look down on anyone who is a born-again child of God because you will wake up one day to see that individual at the very top. Christians are going to command enormous wealth in this end time. Therefore, you must position yourself as a child of God because the time has come for you to take charge.

It is interesting for children of God to note that the wealth being released in this end time is not for every child of God but those who walk in the covenant. It will be surprising that some children of God will be spectators of this end-time transfer of wealth. God's prosperity plan is a covenant, and until you walk in the light of that covenant, you will never partake of his wealth. The release of wealth in this end time is to compensate God's children who have been obedient to the demands of covenant walk, not covenant talk. This end time wealth will clearly distinguish those who have been walking with God by following his instruction.

> *Then shall ye return, and discern between the righteous and the wicked, between him that serveth God and him that serveth him not.*
> MALACHI 3:18

When we quote the above Scripture, we take it to mean that God will make a separation between his children and the children of the world, it is true, but the last statement is also for the church. There will be a clear distinction even in the body of Christ between those who truly serve God and those who just go to church. There are those who are title holders in the church but are not God's servant. The coming wealth transfer is to make everyone see and know that God rewards those who serve him. In my local church, there is a pastor friend who has started to experience this wealth transfer. This pastor just bought a house meant for millionaires and celebrities at a ridiculous amount. The property is so huge that everyone who went to see the house is still struggling to come to terms that he actually owns the house. Children of God, let it be known to you that it has not started yet, great things are coming. All the prayers you have been praying and all your labors of love in God's Kingdom will be rewarded in this season of wealth transfer. We are in the era of the restoration of all things. It is the time for the restoration of the dignity of the believers. All the years that the enemy has cheated you out of your right are going to be restored now. If you have ever sowed in tears, it is time to reap with joy.

> *He that goeth forth and weepeth,*
> *bearing precious seed,*
> *shall doubtless come again with rejoicing,*
> *bringing his sheaves with him.*
> PSALM 126:6

Some people argue that it is not good that a child of God should be wealthy. This is a foolish argument because poverty is an assault on redemption, and Jesus died to connect us to the blessings of Abraham. He also died to receive unto us riches, and the Bible says that though he was rich yet, he became poor so that through his poverty we might become rich. Poverty is not a criterion for making it to heaven, and if any believer dies poor, it means that believer did not appropriate the redemptive package that Jesus died for. What a shame.

> *Then said I, Wisdom is better*
> *than strength: nevertheless the*
> *poor man's wisdom is despised,*
> *and his words are not heard.*
> ECCLESIASTES 9:16

Poverty is an abuse on redemption. If you are poor, no one will want to identify with you, no matter how wise you might be. If you go to tell someone that God is good, then you must look good yourself. People will follow you if they see the reflection of what you are talking about in you. Many believers attribute wealth to the people in the world, and they come up with many distorted quotes like "it is difficult for a rich man to make heaven." God wants his children to be wealthy, and that is why he wants to repeat what he did in Egypt by transferring the wealth of the world to his faithful servants.

To be a part of the wealth transfer season, you must engage in the covenant of seed time and harvest, and the foremost in that covenant is tithe. Faithful tithers will experience wealth never recorded in the history of their families. Many believers will touch the kind of wealth that if Jesus tarry, generations yet unborn will feel the effect of it. Therefore, let every child of God be up and doing, engage in endeavors as directed by God, and you shall soon take over.

CHAPTER 9

PROSPERITY OF THE CHURCH

Anchor Scripture:

Cry yet, saying, Thus saith the Lord of hosts; My cities through prosperity shall yet be spread abroad; and the Lord shall yet comfort Zion, and shall yet choose Jerusalem.

Zachariah 1:17

GLOBAL HOLOCAUST

WE ARE IN THE GOLDEN ERA OF THE CHURCH.

We are truly in the era of the church. Churches are becoming like nations and are spreading like wildfire, and no government or powers can stop them. The anchor Scripture for this chapter says that the Kingdom of God will spread abroad through prosperity. The kingdom of this world shall become the Kingdom of God and of Christ, and we will see it with our eyes as God prospers the church and makes her to take over everywhere.

In our time, we are seeing churches becoming the leading institutions in the world. Most of the best hospitals are owned by churches as are many educational institutions. Churches are now funding research projects across the globe. The time when churches used to look like abandoned shrines is over as we have seen churches holding services in great edifices boasting architectural wonders. Despite all these feats so far, God's church is about to experience great prosperity as never known in history. For the gospel of Christ to reach every soul, and for the end to come, the church must be prosperous to achieve it. Jesus is coming to meet a prosperous church. God's church will soon become the most powerful institution on the earth. Before Jesus left, he told the church to occupy till He comes,

> *And he called his ten servants,*
> *and delivered them ten pounds,*
> *and said unto them, Occupy till I come.*
> LUKE 19:13

The word occupy as used here means to "take charge." For many years God's church did not take charge but was at the mercy of the people. Recently we have seen the rise of the church to the position that Jesus expected it to be, and soon the church will take over. The church is beginning to break forth on every side. The time is coming when the government will depend on the church. God's church will rule in every area of life. The Master said the church should occupy and so she must occupy in creating jobs, establishing schools, and building hospitals while the government is busy building prisons and rehabilitation centers. The church must occupy the entire system because the Master must return to see his bride in charge.

GLOBAL HOLOCAUST

And the seventh angel sounded; and there were great voices in heaven, saying, The kingdoms of this world are become the kingdoms of our Lord, and of his Christ; and he shall reign for ever and ever.
REVELATION 11:15

The church should not be frightened or pushed into a corner of insignificance but must rise and rule because the kingdom of this world has become the kingdom of our Lord Jesus. There is a release of supernatural wealth upon the church of the end time, and this wealth will increase the church and make it the most powerful institution. Therefore, let the body of Christ arise out of obscurity and begin to dominate wherever they are found. To engage in any kingdom project, the church needs finances. Therefore, the release of this wealth is to help the church fulfill its mandate on the earth. The church is not to hoard the wealth but to use it to serve the needs of humanity. Therefore, let every church begin to see what area they can function and use God's given resources in that particular area. The church should build schools to help those who cannot afford the high cost of education, and build hospitals to help the needy in the community where they are found.

> *And in the days of these kings shall the God of heaven set up a kingdom, which shall never be destroyed: and the kingdom shall not be left to other people, but it shall break in pieces and consume all these kingdoms, and it shall stand for ever.*
> DANIEL 2:44

The church has been set up by God and not by man. The church is destined to outlast every other institution and government on the earth. And it is written that the church cannot be destroyed no matter how hard anyone tries to destroy it. As an everlasting institution, the church should take precedence. God has designed the church to rule, and He is releasing resources to help her rule. Therefore, don't be amazed at how prosperous the church has become because it is the agenda of heaven. Instead, rush into the flow and make an impact, for it is the era of the church.

> *Beloved, I wish above all things that thou mayest prosper and be in health, even as thy soul prospereth.*
> 3 JOHN 1:2

It is God's intent that the church prospers. Over the years, from the onset, the church has been spiritually prosperous, but it is time that the church not only prospers spiritually but materially. You cannot successfully run a gospel mission without resources, and it is a sin for Christians to beg or borrow from the people in the world to fund the agenda of God. The whole resources of the earth belong to God and for the church to beg for help from unbelievers is the highest insult to the person of the Most High God.

> *The silver is mine, and the gold is mine, saith the Lord of hosts.*
> HAGGAI 2:8

The bank of heaven is never depleted. The prosperity of the church in this end time will baffle the world as the church will command enormous wealth. The time for begging and borrowing is over and the time for churches to lend to many nations has come. Countries will run to the church for bailouts, and many institutions in the world will go to the church for help both spiritually and financially. It is the era of the prosperity of the church. Glory be to God.

CHAPTER 10

PERSECUTION OF THE CHURCH

Anchor Scripture:

Then shall they deliver you up to be afflicted, and shall kill you: and ye shall be hated of all nations for my name's sake.

Matthew 24:9

GLOBAL HOLOCAUST

THERE IS COMING A GREAT PERSECUTION UPON CHRIST'S CHURCH.

I switched on my TV one day and saw a group of Christians gathered in front of a building and protesting about religious liberty, and I told someone who was with me that "it has not started yet." The church will face great persecution very soon. Recently we have seen in the United States and other parts of the world where morning devotions and prayers have been taken out of school programs because of complaints that it was not an all-inclusive agenda, or it was offensive to people of other religions. A city clerk was arrested because she refused to grant a license to gay couples and the world wondered why. If people have the right to marry whoever they want, then people should also have the right to officiate the marriage they want. I am not against people doing whatever seems right to them, but I strongly believe that right should not have boundaries. The recent happenings in America and other parts of the world should make Christians sit up and be prayerful because great persecution is coming to the church. Christian beliefs are in jeopardy and soon born-again Christians will become endangered species.

> *And Saul was consenting unto his death. And at that time there was a great persecution against the church which was at Jerusalem; and they were all scattered abroad throughout the regions of Judaea and Samaria, except the apostles.*
> ACTS 8:1

The persecution of the church did not start today but dates back to the time of the apostles. It was persecution that scattered the church abroad as stated in the above Scripture and after that came the greatest of them during the reign of Nero, the sixth emperor of Rome, who persecuted the church so much that he burnt Christians at the stake to light his garden. Over the years, leaders of nations have sought to destroy the church. We know that humans are not the true persecutors of the church but the devil himself. Satan has vowed to exterminate the body of Christ so that the returned Messiah will not find his bride on the earth. We know the devil cannot succeed, because no matter what the enemy does, the church of Jesus is more than a conqueror.

> *Who shall separate us from the love of Christ? shall tribulation, or distress, or persecution, or famine, or nakedness, or peril, or sword? As it is written, For thy sake we are killed all the day long; we are accounted as sheep for the slaughter. Nay, in all these things we are more than conquerors through him that loved us.*
> ROMANS 8:35-37

When the world sees how prosperous the church has become, and the influx of multitudes into the church, this will stir envy in the hearts of evil men, and they will rise to persecute the church of Jesus. God's church will face great persecution as never recorded in history. Recently we have seen people enter churches and kill worshipers. We have also seen in some parts of the world where suicide bombers have targeted churches. Many churches have been burned down by arsonists, and we ask why. There is coming great persecution, and the church should brace up for it because the enemy is bent on destroying God's church through his human agents.

> *For we wrestle not against flesh and blood, but against principalities, against powers, against the rulers of the darkness of this world, against spiritual wickedness in high places.*
> EPHESIANS 6:12

The church is fighting her last spiritual battle, and it is a fight to the death. The enemy is bent on winning, and will not give up. That is why we see so many assaults against the church. The gates of hell are launching the deadliest assault against the body of Christ as never seen in history so the church must brace up for what is about to come. There is a serious plan from the pit of hell against the church. Therefore, children of God must put on the whole armor and be ready for battle.

> *Wherefore take unto you the whole armour of God, that ye may be able to withstand in the evil day, and having done all, to stand.*
> EPHESIANS 6:13

GLOBAL HOLOCAUST

I believe the church must begin to be on the offensive now and not wait until when there is trouble. That is when frantic prayers begin to ascend to heaven. The church must be on alert and be prepared to withstand the devil and his assaults. The time is coming when born-again Christians will become endangered species. There is coming a great persecution upon the church. The after effect of wealth transfer upon the children of God and the prosperity of the church, which made the church become the most powerful institution, will be the persecution of the church. Great persecution is coming to the church. Governments, individuals, and organizations will soon rise against the church. The time is coming when people will seek legislation to make the church pay taxes. Many governments of nations will ask churches and their pastors to acquire a license before they operate and if you are caught operating or preaching without a license, it will amount to arrest and prosecution. Born-again Christians will soon be branded as extremists even by other church denominations. Men of the underworld will infiltrate the church to find occasion to bring it down. The time is coming when in some part of the world, local authorities, out of envy, will use force to close some churches. The time is coming when anyone who kills a Christian will think that he does service to God.

> *They shall put you out of the synagogues: yea, the time cometh, that whosoever killeth you will think that he doeth God service.*
> JOHN 16:2

Jesus said that Christians will be delivered up to be killed, and we see that happening even now. It is important to know that the greatest persecution of the church will come from the church, and those in danger of persecution are those labeled fanatics. Those fanatics will be true born-again Christians. When Jesus came into this world, those who rose against Him were not government authorities but the religious leaders. Therefore, no matter how non-Christians are killing Christians now in the name of religion, the greatest persecution will come from Christian religious leaders of our time. Those who think that they are holding the position of Christ on the earth are the same people who will persecute the supposed Christian extremists, just like those who were defending the laws of God were the same people who killed Christ.

Then shall they deliver you up to be afflicted, and shall kill you: and ye shall be hated of all nations for my name's sake.
MATTHEW 24:9

The time is coming when Christians will betray Christians, they shall be informants to the authorities and will give many up to be jailed and killed. Soon many people will openly show their hatred for Christians without just cause. This is not the time for born-again Christians to slumber or be lukewarm. What is coming is great and we must begin to fight on our knees so that when trouble comes, we had stored up enough power to withstand the enemy.

CHAPTER 11

GREAT FALLING AWAY OF BELIEVERS

ANCHOR SCRIPTURE:

Let no man deceive you by any means: for that day shall not come, except there come a falling away first, and that man of sin be revealed, the son of perdition;

2 THESSALONIANS 2:3

THERE SHALL BE GREAT FALLING AWAY OF BELIEVERS IN THIS END TIME.

Before the coming of Jesus, there shall be a great falling away of believers. There are factors that will cause many Christians to fall away from the faith, and by the help of the Holy Spirit, we will look at a few of those factors.

UNBELIEF

During the earthly ministry of Jesus, many of his disciples were offended in him because of what he said and stopped following him, and he turned to the twelve and asked them if they wanted to leave also.

> *From that time many of his disciples went back, and walked no more with him. Then said Jesus unto the twelve, Will ye also go away?*
> JOHN 6:66-67

Just like in the time of Jesus, many believers will be offended and leave. They will no longer believe the Word of God. Many who are burning with fire for the Lord will soon drop out of the race. Their hearts will no longer heed to the teachings of Christ, and every word of God will lose meaning to their ears.

DISOBEDIENCE

Another reason why many will fall from the faith will be disobedience. Many believers who disobey God and refuse to serve God with their resources will fall away from the faith. They will see covenant Christians prospering during the wealth transfer, and become offended that they don't share that circumstance. They will leave Jesus and seek prosperity from other sources. We know what happens to those who go to others for help.

> *Woe to them that go down to Egypt for help; and stay on horses, and trust in chariots, because they are many; and in horsemen, because they are very strong; but they look not unto the Holy One of Israel, neither seek the Lord!*
> ISAIAH 31:1

GLOBAL HOLOCAUST

I believe it is easier to obey God and do what He tells you rather than to stay in disobedience and when things don't work as planned, blame him and abandon him and go to another. In doing this, you are not helping yourself, instead you bring a curse upon your life and those who depend on you. God will never need any man for anything; it is man who needs God for everything. You see, it is not about holding title or being filled with religious activities that qualify us for the blessing. Covenant wealth is a walk, and if you don't have this walk with God, you are not qualified for kingdom wealth.

CARES OF THIS WORLD

Many people who are serving God now will soon be carried away by the cares of this world and thus, will fall away from the faith. Even though we see them in church every day, the Word of God does not have root in their hearts, and it will soon show.

> *And these are they which are sown among thorns; such as hear the word, And the cares of this world, and the*

> *deceitfulness of riches, and the lusts of other things entering in, choke the word, and it becometh unfruitful.*
> MARK 4:18-19

These are people who hear the Word of God in every service and they are part of every activity in church, but will soon be carried away by what they see happening in the world. Because they want to be like the people of the world, they will fall away. They want to drive the fanciest cars and live in mansions like others they see. They want their children to attend the best schools, and they also want to be recognized and seen as successful. They will not want to wait for God but will forsake Christ because the Word of God did not have root in their hearts.

PRIDE

Some of those who begin to experience true prosperity because of the wealth transfer will swell with pride, and the blessing of wealth will take them away from the faith. You see many people who are serving the Lord faithfully now are doing so because of the state they are in. When the blessing comes, their true characters will be revealed. If you want to know the true character of a man, give him wealth.

> *And thou say in thine heart,*
> *My power and the might of mine*
> *hand hath gotten me this wealth.*
> DEUTERONOMY 8:17

God warns against pride after receiving the blessing. Many people will claim that it is because of their efforts and possibly their intelligence and hard work that have brought them the wealth. And because they refuse to see God as the one who gave them the wealth, they will leave the church and go to join cults to be among the elite and to protect their wealth, and this will lead to their destruction.

NEWFOUND FAITH

Many believers will soon leave the faith because of new doctrines. Many children of God have already abandoned their faith for the New Age Movement, without knowing that these are doctrines of the devil aimed at distracting people from God to their own destruction.

Now the Spirit speaketh expressly, that in the latter times some shall depart from the faith, giving heed to seducing spirits, and doctrines of devils;
1 TIMOTHY 4:1

The New Age Movement and other doctrines of evil are gaining momentum as the devil is using them to sway children of God away from the faith in Jesus Christ. These newfound faiths will lead many to hell, and believers who abandon the doctrine of Jesus to these new doctrines will find it difficult to come back to Jesus.

For it is impossible for those who were once enlightened, and have tasted of the heavenly gift, and were made partakers of the Holy Ghost, And have tasted the good word of God, and the powers of the world to come, If they shall fall away, to renew them again unto repentance; seeing they crucify to themselves the Son of God afresh, and put him to an open shame.
HEBREWS 6:4-6

GLOBAL HOLOCAUST

The Spirit of God has made it clear that in the latter times (which is now), many shall depart from the faith. The great falling away of believers is something that has been ordained to happen, and the only way out is to be grounded in God. The Scripture says that the reason many will leave the faith is because they will give heed to seducing spirits and doctrines of devils. We have so many religions that people feel there is no difference anymore; they will say, "Are we not all Christians?" No, we are not all Christians, there is no such thing as Christian science. Any spirit that does not glorify Jesus as Lord is not from God. Many believers will be carried away by new age doctrines without knowing that they are the doctrines of devils. A Christian brother left our church some time ago, and when I made contact with him, he said to me that he was now worshiping where the richest people in the land were worshiping and that he had just found the light. Little did he know that the newfound light was actually darkness. Any light that contradicts the Scripture of truth is darkness in disguise. We should remember that the devil can transform into an angel of light. All of a sudden, things started turning upside down for this friend of mine; he lost virtually everything. You can't come to Jesus and lose things to a point of losing your life, no, God decorates, He doesn't bring people down. Many people in these last days will be influenced by seducing spirits. The Bible calls them seducing spirits because their plan is to lure people out from the faith so they can be destroyed. The kingdom of darkness is out in full force in this end time. Lying spirits are out to destroy many souls. They lure believers from the truth that they already know by presenting something close to it which are but lies.

PERSECUTION

Persecution of Christians is one thing that will cause many to run away from Jesus, especially those who were grounded and at the forefront of the gospel.

> *And these are they likewise which are sown on stony ground; who, when they have heard the word, immediately receive it with gladness; And have no root in themselves, and so endure but*

> *for a time: afterward, when affliction or persecution ariseth for the word's sake, immediately they are offended.*
> MARK 4:16-17

The Bible says that these people will run away from the faith not because they did not love Jesus but because the Word of God, although they received it with gladness, fell on stony ground. And because the Word of God does not have root in their hearts, when afflictions arise because of the Word, they will leave the church. When they hear of the beheading of Christians, they denounce Jesus and refuse to identify with anyone who is a Christian for fear that calamity will come upon them. Persecution of Christians in this end time will cause many who love their lives too much to stop identifying with Christ. When people start laughing at those who are born-again Christians, many will throw their Bibles away and stop going for fellowship so that they will not be seen as belonging to Christ.

In this end time, many great ministers will fall from grace; many will be discouraged while others will be ashamed of following Jesus. The world will witness many great men of God denouncing Jesus because of one thing or the other. This should not make anyone afraid, but should strengthen the believers because the Bible made it clear that this must happen before the end.

> *Let no man deceive you by any means: for that day shall not come, except there come a falling away first, and that man of sin be revealed, the son of perdition;*
> 2 THESSALONIANS 2:3

It is expressly written that the end will not come except many people falls away from the faith. Therefore, let those who are grounded in Christ have nothing to fear but when you see this happening, know that the end is near, even at the door.

CHAPTER 12

THE NATION OF ISRAEL AND MIDDLE EAST CRISIS

Anchor Scripture:

And the dragon was wroth with the woman, and went to make war with the remnant of her seed, which keep the commandments of God, and have the testimony of Jesus Christ.

Revelation 12:17

THE MIDDLE EAST CRISIS IS MORE OF A SPIRITUAL CONFLICT.

The crisis in the Middle East did not start today. There had been conflicts since the children of Israel stepped into their present land. The reason why there are problems in the Middle East is far from human comprehension. It is a struggle between the forces of good and evil. There is nothing any man or organization can do to stop the Middle East conflict. It has been, and it will continue to a final breakdown that will bring about the destruction of man and the earth.

The children of Israel are the chosen people of God. Jesus, the Messiah of man, came from Israel. Even before Jesus came, the devil was fighting the children of Israel by trying to annihilate them. The devil wanted to stop the plan and purpose of God to bring the Messiah, who will save man and reconcile him back to God. The devil did not want that to come to pass. When the enemy could not succeed and the Messiah came, the devil planned with the religious people of that time to kill Jesus. The devil did not want God's plan to succeed. It was foolish, because by killing Jesus, God's plan was made manifest.

> *Which none of the princes of this world knew: for had they known it, they would not have crucified the Lord of glory.*
> 1 CORINTHIANS 2:8

When the devil saw that he could not succeed and his plan failed, he heated up his attack on Israel. He pitched nations against them to destroy them but the amazing thing is that as tiny a nation as Israel is, they cannot be destroyed. Hitler tried it but could not succeed. The Six-Day War is a clear example that the nation of Israel cannot be destroyed. No matter who gangs up against the children of Israel, God protects his chosen people and they are indestructible.

Many people think that the Middle East crisis will cause a nuclear holocaust. Yes, it is true but not until the rapture. There is no cause for fear no matter how many nuclear weapons Israel's enemies acquire. There will be no nuclear war now until the rapture happens. There might be peace in the Middle East if the children of Israel gave up their land and moved from the spot they are in now as a nation. We know that will not happen because God gave the Israelites the land and no matter how the devil fights, he cannot displace Israel.

I said in a preceding chapter that the most contested piece of land on earth is the land of Israel, and Jerusalem is the center of it. The Temple Mount is the boiling pot of the contest. The devil thought he had succeeded by pitching the Dome of the Rock mosque, but he is still not happy. No matter how many countries hates Israel, their God is too strong for anyone to destroy them. The only thing that those who loves and support Israel should do is to continue to pray for them because the Middle East crisis will continue until Jesus comes. Israel is the physical representation of the rule of God on the earth, and an attempt to destroy Israel is an attempt to destroy God, and even the devil knows that it is impossible.

GOD'S PROMISE TO THE JEWS

Every promise of God to the Jews will find express fulfillment before the end comes. God promised that He would bring them again to their land, and He did just that in 1948.

> *For I will set mine eyes upon them*
> *for good, and I will bring them again*
> *to this land: and I will build them,*
> *and not pull them down; and I will*
> *plant them, and not pluck them up.*
> JEREMIAH 24:6

As the Almighty promised to settle the children of Israel in their land, so has He fulfill it to the amazement of the entire world. This shows that every Word of God and every promise of God to the children of Israel will be fulfilled to the letter. God does not make empty promises, whatever He says that is what He will do whether to a man or a nation. You can rest assured that when God make a promise, that He will do it, no matter how long it takes. His Word must come to pass. When God promised to deliver the children of Israel from bondage in Egypt, the devil fought to stop the promise. When the time came, God used a man raised in the house of the people who oppressed the Israelites to deliver them. Likewise, as God promised that the son of David would sit on the throne of his father in Israel, then we must know that it will surely come to pass.

> *And, behold, thou shalt conceive in thy womb, and bring forth a son, and shalt call his name Jesus. He shall be great, and shall be called the Son of the Highest: and the Lord God shall give unto him the throne of his father David: And he shall reign over the house of Jacob for ever; and of his kingdom there shall be no end.*
> LUKE 1:31-33

God has promised that the son of David, an Israelite, will sit on the throne of his father and He shall reign over Israel forever. This mean that the nation of Israel will continue and that an Israeli king will rule over the whole earth. Jesus, who is the Messiah, is destined to rule over Israel and the entire nations of the earth and this promise of God to the Jews will surely happen. The Jews should believe this promise of God and prepare themselves to receive the Messiah, who will arrive any moment from now. Jesus is coming soon, and his coming is to fulfill the promise of God to the Jews and to all who believe in him.

CHAPTER 13

ERA OF FALSE PROPHETS

Anchor Scripture:

For there shall arise false Christs, and false prophets, and shall shew great signs and wonders; insomuch that, if it were possible, they shall deceive the very elect.

Matthew 24:24

WE ARE LIVING IN THE VERY ERA OF FALSE PROPHETS.

The Scriptures have never been fulfilled as they will be before our very eyes in these last days. Without contradiction, we are living in the era of false prophets. There has been the rise of many who claim to be the Messiah, and I had been a student of one of such. There is a great rise of many false prophets who come in the name of the Lord as Jesus predicted. These false prophets come, doing great miracles signs and wonders that many believers have been drawn to them by their deceit. It is good for children of God to read the Bible so that they can know and be wary of deception. Many of these false prophets have swindle people of their wealth while others have destroyed the souls of many. Jesus warns us to be careful and not to listen to these false prophets because they are dangerous.

Many false prophets draw their power from the devil who gives them such power so they can deceive many people to hell. These prophets cause deceitful prophecies in church and strange manifestations in their congregations making people believe it is God at work.

When you meet with these false prophets, they can tell everything about you that will make you wonder how they got to know, and in so doing you will think it is the Spirit of God, not knowing it is of the devil. The Spirit of God will never begin to tell you of your past, neither will it tell you your future. Any spirit that foretells is evil, and is called a familiar spirit. Of such run away because it will hook you on lies through the telling of your past and you will never see the light except by grace.

And it came to pass, as we went to prayer, a certain damsel possessed with a spirit of divination met us, which brought her masters much gain by soothsaying:
ACTS 16:16

There is a great release of the spirit of deception into the world in these last days, and false prophets are personified carriers of such spirits, working for their master the devil. I saw a video of a so-called prophet being carried on a chair by members while preaching saying that his legs must not touch the ground while he preached. That was demonic. Children of God must be careful as not to listen or be drawn into such grand deceit.

There are many false prophets operating in the world, and more are coming. Jesus said that they will show great signs and wonders, so be careful when you hear that there is a prophet in town who can make your problems go away instantly. I saw a church where the pastor asked their members to bring out their phones to receive miracle calls, Those phones began to ring right in the church. What he said came true, but know that it was not from God because the Spirit of God does work that way, neither is God a magician.

> *Wherefore if they shall say unto you, Behold, he is in the desert; go not forth: behold, he is in the secret chambers; believe it not.*
> MATTHEW 24:26

True breakthrough comes from God after you have received his son Jesus as your Lord and Savior. Healing and deliverance are for God's children, although nonbelievers can have the crumbs according to the mercy of God for the sole purpose of showing his power so that the unbeliever can believe. Any gathering where the true Word of God is not preached, and sinners are led to Christ but abound in miracles signs and wonders is not of God. Anywhere you are asked to bring money for prayers is not a good place, healing and deliverance from God are not for sale but freely given.

> *Heal the sick, cleanse the lepers,*
> *raise the dead, cast out devils:*
> *freely ye have received, freely give.*
> MATTHEW 10:8

Miracles are not for sale. Wherever you are asked to pay money before your problems are solved is the den of false prophets. The Holy Spirit does not charge for healing or deliverance. Many false prophets enter into the business of miracles for sale so they can make wealth. Because their desires are for worldly gain, they get supernatural powers from the devil to get a crowd of people into their church and get rich in the process. If you want to know these false prophets, listen to their messages. They can't preach a simple message that will make sinners repent. The rise of false prophets in this end time is orchestrated by the devil so that he can lead many to hell.

CHAPTER 14

AMERICA IN GOD'S END TIME AGENDA

IT IS MY OPINION THAT THE UNITED STATES OF AMERICA WILL PLAY A VITAL ROLE IN FULFILLING GOD'S END TIME PLAN.

This chapter is my opinion. America is a country chosen by God. Throughout the history of the United States, we have seen that it took only the hand of God to carve out the nation. Reading the history of United States of America is fascinating because there is proof that God brought the nation to fulfill His purposes on the earth. Sometimes I wonder if there was no America what might happen on this earth today. The blessings of America are not brought about by human hands, and no one can claim to be responsible for them.

The United States is the only country in this world that was founded upon biblical principles and as their popular phrase could tell, "One nation under God" and "In God we trust." God is the founder and the foundation of the United States of America, and that is why she has been on the forefront of championing the cause of the gospel. Many nations of the world depend on the USA for help and concerning global issues. If the USA does not initiate or lead, then there is a problem, as in the case of climate change.

Many Christian ministries in the world depended on the United States for support and years ago, if you wanted to succeed in moving your ministry forward, you had to get help from the USA. The United States of America has been a leading force in foreign missions and in helping to spread the gospel to the heathen nations of the world. Without the United States, many countries would not hear the gospel today. Globally, the USA has been a great help.

If the United States had not entered World War II, we don't know what would have happened. If not for America, who has been a great supporter of Israel, we don't know what would happen to them today. America is the largest donor of medicines globally, and the greatest humanitarian help to countries in crisis comes from the USA. In the United States, it seems like a noble thing to do for those who have made it in life to share their fortunes by providing humanitarian aid to underprivileged people around the world as we see the richest men in the world and celebrities doing often.

When the wind of revival hit America years back, the world felt it as American missionaries traveled around the world to share the fire of such revival. Some of the world's greatest evangelists are from America, and this will help buttress the fact that God founded America to help fulfill his purpose. America is a Christian nation founded on Christian principles. It is this foundation that has made the United States the greatest, most powerful, and the richest nation on the earth. Because of the prosperity of the USA, many people from around the world left their countries to come and settle in America. It is foolishness, therefore, to allow people who have fled their countries to come in and pollute America in the name of liberty.

As we have seen in times past, America is going to play a vital role in ushering in the government of our Lord Jesus Christ; that is why the United States of America should not allow outsiders to come in and spoil their country for them. Christianity is what makes

America great and only a fool would deny that. Others saw the prosperity in America and decided to come and live in America in order to share in her blessings. And when they came in, they wanted to spoil the country by demanding ridiculous changes that would ruin the country. How can someone try to stop prayers in school saying that it is not all-inclusive and that prayers are offensive to their own religion, and the government listens to them? Is it not the same prayer that made America blessed and they left their own country for it? If Americans are not careful, people will come in and spoil their country for them. In as much as everyone is welcome, the basic principles upon which the country was founded should not be compromised. You did something that made your country great and that greatness attracted different kinds of people to you. When those people came in, they demanded for their convenience that you change those things which made you great. Don't you think that would be disastrous? If God is removed from American schools and other institutions, then America will be heading for a fall. America should remember that God is their trust and when they leave

God in order not to hurt people's feeling, then God will leave them.

In this end time, Israel needs America, and I ask America to strengthen their diplomatic ties with Israel, and they should do that as quickly as possible. Israel is the best ally America can get, and I tell you the truth, if America has only Israel as their ally, let the whole world come against America, they won't be able to destroy it. Israel is the home of God's chosen people, and with God on your side, one is a majority.

CHAPTER 15

NIGERIA, A NATION TO WATCH

Anchor Scripture:

Then Peter opened his mouth, and said, Of a truth I perceive that God is no respecter of persons: But in every nation he that feareth him, and worketh righteousness, is accepted with him.

Acts 10:34-35

NIGERIA IS A NATION TO WATCH OUT FOR IN THIS END TIME.

The information in this chapter is my personal opinion. I am from Nigeria and believe that Nigeria is the greatest and most populous black nation in the world. With a population of about one hundred and eighty-one million, Nigeria stands as a very significant country in the comity of nations. In this end time, I believe Nigeria will play a very vital role in the move of God and fulfill his plan. It is my opinion that that the greatest things in the gospel in these last hours are happening in Nigeria. The greatest names in the gospel that are making an impact around the world now are from Nigeria.

The largest church auditorium ever built and without pillars with a capacity to seat fifty thousand people is in Nigeria. This church runs four services, and all the services are full to the brim. This is not recorded anywhere else in the world. It is important to note that pastors of the church constructed the building without any foreign expertise, contractors, or financial contributions. It was completed within one year and is debt free, to the amazement of the entire world. The name of the church is *Living Faith Church*, also known as *Winners Chapel International*, situated in Ota, Africa; otherwise called Canaanland, founded by Bishop David Oyedepo.

> *But God hath chosen the foolish things of the world to confound the wise; and God hath chosen the weak things of the world to confound the things which are mighty;*
> 1 CORINTHIANS 1:27

God in His wisdom chose the most unlikely people to showcase his power and glory in this end time, a class of people not regarded by others. Bishop David Oyedepo and Winners Chapel leads me to believe that Nigeria is at the very center of God's agenda in this end time. A single church built this structure, and not only that, they turned a forest into a city that attracts everyone from around the world. That is proof of God's power. It is important to bring to record that not only was the church built in one year, but the university that is in the church was built in seven months. God is moving in this end time, and Nigeria is part of that movement with many recorded feats.

Among the greatest things happening in the gospel is the largest church gathering in the world and this is only recorded in Nigeria. It is the *Redeemed Christian Church of God* monthly Holy Ghost Congress. It is a monthly gathering of the Saints at the Redemption Camp in Nigeria, and it is recorded that over a million people gather there every month. There is nowhere else in the world that has such a number of people gather at once to hear the gospel since Billy Graham's crusade in Seoul, South Korea in 1973, and is presided by Pastor E. E. Adeboye, a man known to have performed uncountable miracles.

The greatest prayer mountain in the world is the Mountain of Fire and Miracle Ministry founded and presided by Dr. Daniel K. Olukoya. It is in this ministry that prayers are offered continually with fervency, and great deliverances are recorded as people from all over the world flock in to be delivered. These ministries and their leaders among others still residing in Nigeria are among the most sought after ministers of the gospel around the world. Their impact has been felt worldwide, and they have helped shape the world spiritually.

Nigeria is a nation to watch in this end time because it is from Nigeria that mantle services, anointing services, feet washing services, and serving of communion in churches became popular in Christian worship centers, which was initially condemned; and all these mysteries were introduced by Bishop David Oyedepo of Winners Chapel, as instructed by the Holy Spirit. If God decided to introduce mysteries of the Kingdom to his servants from Nigeria, that could mean Nigeria is in God's end time plan. If that is the case, the agenda of God's plan for this end time in preparing the Saints for rapture could come from Nigeria. We must understand that God is no respecter of persons according to the anchor Scripture, and if the men of God in Nigeria have sold themselves out to the things of the Kingdom of God, that means God is willing to work with them to prove Himself. It is time for the children of God from around the world to keep a keen eye on the nation of Nigeria because I believe the unfolding of the end time plan will include Nigeria.

*And many people shall go and say,
Come ye, and let us go up to the mountain
of the Lord, to the house of the God of
Jacob; and he will teach us of his ways,
and we will walk in his paths: for out
of Zion shall go forth the law, and the
word of the Lord from Jerusalem.*
Isaiah 2:3

Many of the great evangelists of the end time will come from Nigeria, great men of the Spirit who will work miracles signs, and wonder that will draw multitudes into the Kingdom. Let everyone watch out, for Nigeria could be a major player in advancing the gospel of Jesus Christ in this end time.

CHAPTER 16

FULFILLMENT OF BIBLICAL PROPHECIES

Anchor Scripture:

Heaven and earth shall pass away, but my words shall not pass away.
Matthew 24:35

GLOBAL HOLOCAUST

GOD IS NOT A JOKER, HE SAYS WHAT HE MEANS AND HE MEANS WHAT HE SAYS.

God's word is immutable. That means the Word of God cannot change. Time cannot change the purpose of God and whatever God says, rest assured that no matter how long it takes, His Word must surely come to pass. The Bible is a book full of prophecies about things that will happen, and we are in the era where Bible prophecies are being fulfilled in unprecedented speed. A good Bible student knows that most of the prophecies as foretold in the Scriptures are fulfilled. We have seen many things happen right before our very eyes as prophesied in the Scriptures and this is proof that whatever is yet to happen will happen.

So shall my word be that goeth forth out of my mouth: it shall not return unto me void, but it shall accomplish that which I please, and it shall prosper in the thing whereto I sent it.
ISAIAH 55:11

God's Word cannot return empty, but it must be fulfilled. Many people believe that the world will not end, and some even play on God's mercy by saying that a merciful God will not destroy his creation, so the world will not end. Many religions and even some Christians believe that there is no hell, saying that God is too merciful to create such a hideous place as hell for man.

As humans, we have laws that rule our lives, and for those who break the law, judgment is meted out and can range from incarceration to the death penalty. If man could judge and punish, how about the almighty God, who is the highest authority? Our human explanation cannot cause us to escape from the judgment that will soon come. Instead, we must strive to live right to avoid eternal punishment.

Bible prophecies are being fulfilled in unimaginable speed and every day, we see the truth of the Scriptures staring us in the face. If what was foretold by the prophets and our Lord Jesus Christ have been fulfilled, then we must know that the ones that are yet to be fulfilled will surely come to pass.

GLOBAL HOLOCAUST

But as the days of Noah were, so shall also the coming of the Son of man be. For as in the days that were before the flood they were eating and drinking, marrying and giving in marriage, until the day that Noe entered into the ark, And knew not until the flood came, and took them all away; so shall also the coming of the Son of man be.

MATTHEW 24:37-39

There was a time when the world ended. And before the end, there were prophecies concerning the end and people of that time took the prophecy for granted just like what is happening now. They thought the prophecies were not true, and the world could not end, but to their surprise it ended, and it ended very bad for them. This shows that it is not the first time that the world will end, and so Jesus used that time to warn about what will happen in our own time. He said that just the same way it happened then, it will happen now. We must be wary of every prophecy in the Bible because they are the eternal counsel of God, and they never fail. The people in Noah's time took the Word of God as a joke but at the end the consequences were devastating. Know that every word of prophecy in the Bible will come to pass. Everything that God says He will do, He will do.

It was prophesied that Israel would return to their homeland, and we saw that happened in 1948, as prophesied in the book of Ezekiel 37:21:

And say unto them,
Thus saith the Lord God; Behold,
I will take the children of Israel from
among the heathen, whither they be
gone, and will gather them on every side,
and bring them into their own land:

This prophecy of Ezekiel and others from Isaiah 11:11 and Jeremiah 29:14 is proof of the authenticity of God's Word. The return of the Jewish people to their homeland in Israel is proof that we are in the end time because it was to happen in the last days. This prophecy should act as a wake-up call to everyone alive that every drop of God's Word will be fulfilled and that Jesus the Messiah will return as foretold.

CHAPTER 17

RETURN OF POWER TO ROME

Rome was once the world's superpower, and their control spanned from 31 B.C. to 476 A.D. The Roman Empire with a grip on power for 2,214 years, is one of the longest lasting empires in history. Although Rome fell and for many years lost its political significance, power will return to Rome and this time, it will be both religious and political power.

For a long time now, Rome has exercised a level of control over many nations of the world through the Roman Catholic Church which is presided over by the Pope in the Vatican. The number of Catholics in the world in 2013 was estimated to be over 1.25 billion people. For a religious establishment to have over a billion faithful believers around the world means that they are already an empire and have the capacity to become a world power. This means that the Roman Catholic Church has people in every sphere of endeavor and can easily influence policies.

Religion plays a vital in our lives and over the years we have seen many religious wars and political turmoils in the name of religion. In fact, in some climes, religion plays a vital role in electing political officeholders. Many have killed in the name of religion. If religion carries such influence, then a religious body with over a billion faithfuls can wield enormous power and control in the world. Recently we saw the Pope touring the world. While in America, he was invited to speak at the joint session of Congress; he was also invited to address the United Nations General Assembly, an honor that no other religious leader has enjoyed.

The time is coming when the Roman Catholic Church will take over the whole world, and the Pope will be the head of a one-world government. The journey has started and soon it will become a reality. The government of the world will see the Pope as the most powerful and revered religious leader and will hand over the entire system to his control. Already the Vatican is the 18th richest country in the world although it is the smallest country on earth with no oil wells, gold, or diamond mines yet it controls much riches.

CHAPTER 18

FINALLY THE RAPTURE OF THE CHURCH

ANCHOR SCRIPTURE:

For the Lord himself shall descend from heaven with a shout, with the voice of the archangel, and with the trump of God: and the dead in Christ shall rise first: Then we which are alive and remain shall be caught up together with them in the clouds, to meet the Lord in the air: and so shall we ever be with the Lord. Wherefore comfort one another with these words.

1 THESSALONIANS 4:16-18

RAPTURE IS REAL AND IS ABOUT TO HAPPEN.

The rapture of the church is a topic that is almost not taught in the church today. The church is too busy with so many activities that she almost forgot the reason why she is here and the greatest event of her existence that is about to happen. Many people have come to believe that there is nothing like the rapture and even if it was to happen, the time has passed. But I am here to let you know that the rapture is real and will happen any moment from now. Jesus is coming to take his church away; it is a promise that He made, and his words never fail. Many things that Jesus said would happen have happened, and many are still happening before our very eyes, so what will stop the rapture of the church from taking place?

> *And if I go and prepare a place for you, I will come again, and receive you unto myself; that where I am, there ye may be also.*
>
> JOHN 14:3

Jesus left to go and prepare a place for the church, and He will come again to take the church to the prepared place. It is time the church of the living God begins to teach about the rapture because that is going to be the greatest moment in the life of the church. Without the rapture, the gospel of Jesus has no meaning. God did not allow his son to die so that we would remain in this sinful world. It is the rapture that gives meaning to the death and resurrection of Jesus, and his second coming to earth. Without the rapture, the world would not see any reason why it should accept Jesus. Without the rapture, there is no hope for Christians, so the rapture is very important in the doctrine of Christ and must be given attention especially at this peculiar season.

Let's take a critical look at the Scripture that details the rapture of the church. It says for Jesus Himself will descend from heaven. The devil has been using many people to truncate this truth by claiming that soon there will be alien abduction. There will be no alien abduction but the Lord of the whole earth, the King of Kings, Jesus will come in person to take away the Saints. What is called the rapture is explained by the above Scripture of truth and anyone who says otherwise is a liar. During the rapture, there shall be a shout; we shall hear voices and the sound of the trumpet, and when this happens, the dead in Christ shall rise first. This means that every true born-again Christian that died shall be first to come out of wherever they were buried or wherever they died and no matter the circumstance of their death and no matter how many years they have been dead, they shall come out first. All the Saints from the time Jesus left for heaven up till now will rise from death, and they are the first that shall respond to the voices of the archangels and the trump of God. And after the dead in Christ rise, every born-again Christian that is alive and still standing in faith shall be transformed from the natural sinful earthly body into an incorruptible, supernatural body and that is when they will be able to overcome gravity to join the other risen Saints in the air to meet Jesus.

Let me explain why the dead in Christ will be the first to rise and be raptured. No man can enter heaven with the natural body, and since the dead Saints are already in the grave,

God in his power and wisdom will change their bodies into supernatural bodies and then resurrect them. Because they are already dead, they must be the first to resurrect. Let's see what the Bible says about the souls of those that died.

> *And when he had opened the fifth seal, I saw under the altar the souls of them that were slain for the word of God, and for the testimony which they held: And they cried with a loud voice, saying, How long, O Lord, holy and true, dost thou not judge and avenge our blood on them that dwell on the earth? And white robes were given unto every one of them; and it was said unto them, that they should rest yet for a little season, until their fellowservants also and their brethren, that should be killed as they were, should be fulfilled.*
> REVELATION 6:9-11

Continually in heaven, the souls of the Saints, especially those that were killed for the sake of the gospel are crying out to God for vengeance, and they are being asked to wait a little while. During the rapture, God has to bring them out first to experience the glory of resurrection and rapture, and since we are still alive and are still in the faith, we shall be caught up to join them in meeting with Jesus who will be waiting for the Saints in the air.

The coming of Jesus will not happen at one corner of the earth or in one country where the media has to broadcast live before others can see. During the rapture of the church, the whole world will feel the impact of the event. There shall be commotion everywhere. There shall be plane crashes because if a pilot is born again, when the rapture takes place, that plan is bound to crash. Millions of people will disappear, and all newborn babies and innocent children will disappear from the earth. There will be accidents and heavy traffic across the nations of the earth as born-again drivers will disappear from their car while on the road. It shall be a very glorious moment for every born-again Christian but woe to the world. It shall be a shame to see ministers of the gospel left behind and popular men of God that do not get raptured. The media will call experts to come on live TV to explain the happenings and even call renown pastors and priest who were not raptured to explain what happened. It is then that the world will know that the Christians were truly the light of the world. It is important to know that without you being born again, you cannot experience the rapture.

> *Now this I say, brethren, that flesh and blood cannot inherit the kingdom of God; neither doth corruption inherit incorruption. Behold, I shew you a mystery; We shall not all sleep, but we shall all be changed, In a moment, in the twinkling of an eye, at the last trump: for the trumpet shall sound, and the dead shall be raised incorruptible, and we shall be changed. For this corruptible must put on incorruption, and this mortal must put on immortality. So when this corruptible shall have put on incorruption, and this mortal shall have put on immortality, then shall be brought to pass the saying that is written, Death is swallowed up in victory.*
> 1 CORINTHIANS 15:50-54

This passage gives a clear meaning to my explanation of the rapture. The rapture shall happen in a moment, it shall be so fast that as soon as you hear the sound of the trumpet, you are changed and transported into glory. It is only the dead and living born-again Christians that shall hear the trumpet sound. If you don't hear the trumpet sound, you cannot be raptured.

The mortal body which is flesh and blood cannot enter into heaven. Therefore, it cannot be raptured. Our earthly body is corrupt and to be raptured into glory it must first be changed. When anyone answers the call of salvation and surrenders his or her life to Jesus, at that moment a mystery happens. His old spirit is replaced by a new spirit. That is why it is said that the person is born again, yet his body is still the same. How God does it is a mystery.

The supernatural body enables you to eat, but you don't eat to live, you only eat if you desire to. With this new body, you don't need to take a bath or go to school because you will have supernatural intelligence. You will not need any form of transportation because you will have the ability to be anywhere at the speed of thought. With the new body, you will not have any thought of sin; that is why you can stand in the presence of God. I mean with your glorified body, you will be absolutely pure like Jesus. Jesus is the only man in the Trinity; he can eat, but he does not need to eat to live.

> *But I say unto you, I will not drink henceforth of this fruit of the vine, until that day when I drink it new with you in my Father's kingdom.*
> MATTHEW 26:29

Jesus told his disciples what the new body will be like. He said to them that it would be the last time He would drink this wine with them until He saw them in heaven, then they would drink it new. Jesus can eat and drink, but He has been gone for over two thousand years, yet He hasn't eaten anything, as He waits for us to come before He eats and drinks while celebrating with us.

Oh, if everyone knows the value of the gift of salvation and now that there is time, they would run to Jesus and give their lives to him, so that they can be with him in glory when He appears.

> *Wherefore (as the Holy Ghost saith,*
> *To day if ye will hear his voice,*
> *Harden not your hearts, as in the*
> *provocation, in the day of temptation*
> *in the wilderness: Again, he limiteth a*
> *certain day, saying in David, To day,*
> *after so long a time; as it is said,*
> *To day if ye will hear his voice,*
> *harden not your hearts.*
> HEBREWS 3:7-8, 4:7

Now the Holy Spirit is pleading both with unbelievers and backsliding children of God to return to God and be saved because the hour is near and the trumpet will soon sound.

> *Now then we are ambassadors for*
> *Christ, as though God did beseech*
> *you by us: we pray you in Christ's*
> *stead, be ye reconciled to God.*
> 2 CORINTHIANS 5:20

As an ambassador of Jesus, I join other Saints to plead with you that you give your life to Jesus so that when the trumpet sounds, you will be raptured to heaven to celebrate with Jesus forever. There is nothing in this life and no matter the enjoyment you might think you have here, it cannot be compared to the glory that awaits the Saints in heaven. Please pray this simple prayer after me in the sincerity of your heart and you shall be born again.

Lord Jesus, I come to you.
I know I am a sinner, and I believe you came and died for me that I might be saved. I accept you Jesus as my Lord and Savior. Thank you, Jesus, for forgiving me. Thank you for saving me. Now I know my sins are forgiven. I am saved. I am born again. I am a child of God; old things are passed away and behold all things are become new. In Jesus name, Amen.

Now that you are born again welcome to the body of Christ and continue steadfastly in the faith. Look for a Bible-believing church in your area where the undiluted Word of God is preached and practiced, and serve the Lord Jesus there. If you have difficulty discerning which church is suitable, find Winners Chapel International and attend, and rest assured that when the trumpet sounds, you will be raptured to meet the Lord. God bless you.

CHAPTER 19

ANTICHRIST REVEALED

Anchor Scripture:

And now ye know what withholdeth that he might be revealed in his time. For the mystery of iniquity doth already work: only he who now letteth will let, until he be taken out of the way. And then shall that Wicked be revealed, whom the Lord shall consume with the spirit of his mouth, and shall destroy with the brightness of his coming: Even him, whose coming is after the working of Satan with all power and signs and lying wonders,

2 Thessalonians 2:6-9

GLOBAL HOLOCAUST

The subject of Antichrist has been a controversial issue in the body of Christ. Many argue that the Antichrist has already come and is at work while others say that the Antichrist is the United Nations, and some insinuate that it is the American president. The Bible clearly explains who the Antichrist will be, and I want to tell you that the Antichrist is already available but cannot do anything nor show himself until the time appointed.

The Holy Spirit is the one who is stopping the Antichrist from revealing himself, and until the Holy Spirit is taken away, he will not manifest, according to the anchor Scripture for this chapter. Until the coming of the Antichrist, the process for his manifestation has been going on and it stares us in the face every day, yet many do not know. It is interesting to know that the Antichrist will be the head of the church. The manifestation of the person of the Antichrist depends on when Jesus comes. If Jesus comes now, the person occupying the office will become the Antichrist and if Jesus comes in the next fifty years and the person who occupies that office dies now, the person who will be alive in the capacity of that office at the time will be the Antichrist. The office of the Antichrist is very active now, but the head of that office will only manifest at the time appointed by God. That is why the Bible says that the mystery of iniquity is already at work. It is not something that the world will sleep and wake up one day and a man with two horns on the forehead will take over power and declare himself as the Antichrist. No, but there is a subtle and evil manipulation to install the Antichrist, and it has been going on for a long time.

Let no man deceive you by any means: for that day shall not come, except there come a falling away first, and that man of sin be revealed, the son of perdition; Who opposeth and exalteth himself above all that is called God, or that is worshipped; so that he as God sitteth in the temple of God, shewing himself that he is God.
2 THESSALONIANS 2:3-4

Antichrist means one who is in opposition to Christ. The Antichrist will be the leader of the church. He will sit in the church. The

Bible calls him the man of sin because even though he is the leader of the church, all his conduct is against God. He is also called the son of perdition because he cannot be saved and is meant to be destroyed at the end. Know that the Antichrist will not be the head of the Islam, Buddhist, the United Nations or American President, but like Christ, he will sit in church, oppose and exalt himself above everything that is worshiped. Because he has the backing of Satan, he will perform miracles, signs, and wonders and all the leaders of the world will surrender unto him. He will be the head of one-world government. The Bible says he will show himself as God and because of this the whole world will surrender unto him. It is from his place of power that he will force everyone alive to receive the mark of the beast which is the number of his name before they will be able to buy or sell. As recorded in Revelation 13:16-18:

> *And he causeth all, both small and great,*
> *rich and poor, free and bond,*
> *to receive a mark in their right hand,*
> *or in their foreheads: And that no man*
> *might buy or sell, save he that had the*

mark, or the name of the beast, or the number of his name. Here is wisdom. Let him that hath understanding count the number of the beast: for it is the number of a man; and his number is Six hundred threescore and six.

The Antichrist will rule for seven years with enormous power and great authority and will force everyone to bow down to him or face torture. During his reign, no one will transact any kind of business without having the mark. It shall be a time of great tribulation; the kind the world has never seen. Therefore, one must try everything possible not to be around at that time. The Bible makes it clear that anyone who receives the mark of the beast is in danger of eternal fire (Revelation 20:10). Many people think that the mark of the beast will be 666 written on the palm or the forehead. I believe the Bible says the counting or calculation of the number will result in 666. This means there will be a code, and when you calculate the code, it will give you a total of six hundred and sixty-six. This code will be inserted into the palm of the hand in the form of a microchip or the forehead depending on where you want from either of the two. We have seen it started already, and people are receiving it willingly, but during the reign of the Antichrist it will be by force, and unless you have it, you won't buy or sell.

> *And the king shall do according to his will; and he shall exalt himself, and magnify himself above every god, and shall speak marvellous things against the God of gods, and shall prosper till the indignation be accomplished: for that that is determined shall be done. Neither shall he regard the God of his fathers, nor the desire of women, nor regard any god: for he shall magnify himself above all.*
> DANIEL 11:36-37

When the Supreme Court of the United States of America legalized same-sex marriage, people only saw it as a landmark judgment that gives freedom to people to marry who they want. Little did they know that it was the workings of Satan in preparation for the reign of the Antichrist. The Bible says that the Antichrist will not have any desire for women, which could mean that he will be gay. And so to make it easy for his time, same-sex marriage has to be legalized now. It is easy for me to spot who the Antichrist will be; you don't have to look very far because his office stares us in the face every day. He has been exalting himself above all and also makes utterance that defies God, yet he sits as God in church. May the Lord give you understanding.

CHAPTER 20

THE 144,000 EXPLAINED

ANCHOR SCRIPTURE:

Saying, Hurt not the earth, neither the sea, nor the trees, till we have sealed the servants of our God in their foreheads. And I heard the number of them which were sealed: and there were sealed an hundred and forty and four thousand of all the tribes of the children of Israel. Of the tribe of Juda were sealed twelve thousand. Of the tribe of Reuben were sealed twelve thousand. Of the tribe of Gad were sealed twelve thousand.

REVELATION 7:3-5

GLOBAL HOLOCAUST

The subject of the 144,000 as mentioned in the Bible has been interpreted erroneously by many Christians and even non-Christians who happen to read the Bible. I have read the chapters in the Bible where these mysterious number of people are being mentioned and every time I wonder why it is so difficult for people to understand.

The sealing of the 144,000 is for the children of Israel and not selected people from every part of the world as some people believe. The ones to be sealed are men and not women. If you are waiting to be sealed, you will wait forever because it is for the Jews and not the Gentiles. The Gentiles have been given time to accept Jesus, and those that have not accepted him will go through the tribulation. It is clearly stated in the Scripture the people who are to be sealed and where they are from, according to the anchor Scripture.

The reason why God decided to seal the children of Israel is clearly stated in Revelation 14:3-5.

And they sung as it were a new song before the throne, and before the four beasts, and the elders: and no man could learn that song but the hundred and forty and four thousand, which were redeemed from the earth. These are they which were not defiled with women; for they are virgins. These are they which follow the Lamb whithersoever he goeth. These were redeemed from among men, being the firstfruits unto God and to the Lamb. And in their mouth was found no guile: for they are without fault before the throne of God.

The Bible lists the criteria for sealing those men from the tribes of Israel. It says they will be virgins and ardent followers of Jesus. I believe these people will believe in Jesus, but because they were not born again, they couldn't be raptured. Because they are the chosen people, God decided to redeem them because of their purity and beliefs. Please understand that if you are not born again, you cannot enter heaven. But these people who are to be sealed believe in Jesus and possibly are expecting him to come and so they keep themselves pure and keep every biblical principle thus God decided to redeem them.

The Bible also mentions that those to be sealed are without fault. They kept themselves pure, and before God they were without any sin. It is important to note that the sealing of the 144,000 will take place after the rapture. This means that those to be sealed will not be raptured because if they were raptured, they would not need to be sealed. They will still be here on the earth during the reign of the Antichrist. Therefore, to save them and bring them to heaven, God will seal them. These 144,000 will not receive the mark of the beast. If you read Revelation 7:2-3, you will see that an angel had to stop other angels from hurting the earth until the 144,000 were sealed. I have heard many people say that they are waiting to be sealed. The truth of the Scripture is that Gentiles are not mentioned as part of those who will be sealed. Any Gentile who missed heaven will have his or herself to blame.

It is important for people of God to try and make heaven at the sound of the trumpet. What will happen in this world after the rapture is unimaginable. The devil will rule this earth literally through the Antichrist and to be here in such a time is dangerous. While the Antichrist will make life miserable for people, the Bible says that God will pour out his wrath upon the earth in such a way that people will curse God because of the suffering.

> *And the fourth angel poured out his vial upon the sun; and power was given unto him to scorch men with fire. And men were scorched with great heat, and blasphemed the name of God, which hath power over these plagues: and they repented not to give him glory. And the fifth angel poured out his vial upon the seat of the beast; and his kingdom was full of darkness; and they gnawed their tongues for pain, And blasphemed the God of heaven because of their pains and their sores, and repented not of their deeds.*
> REVELATION 16:8-11

Unbelievable trauma will visit the earth after the rapture as stated in the above Scripture. Therefore, let everyone receive Jesus and keep themselves instead of waiting to be sealed. The

144,000 men to be sealed are Jews and not Gentiles. The sealing of the 144,000 is to keep the devil and the Antichrist from touching them. Therefore, use this grace period which God has given to the Gentiles and prepare to meet with Jesus when He appears.

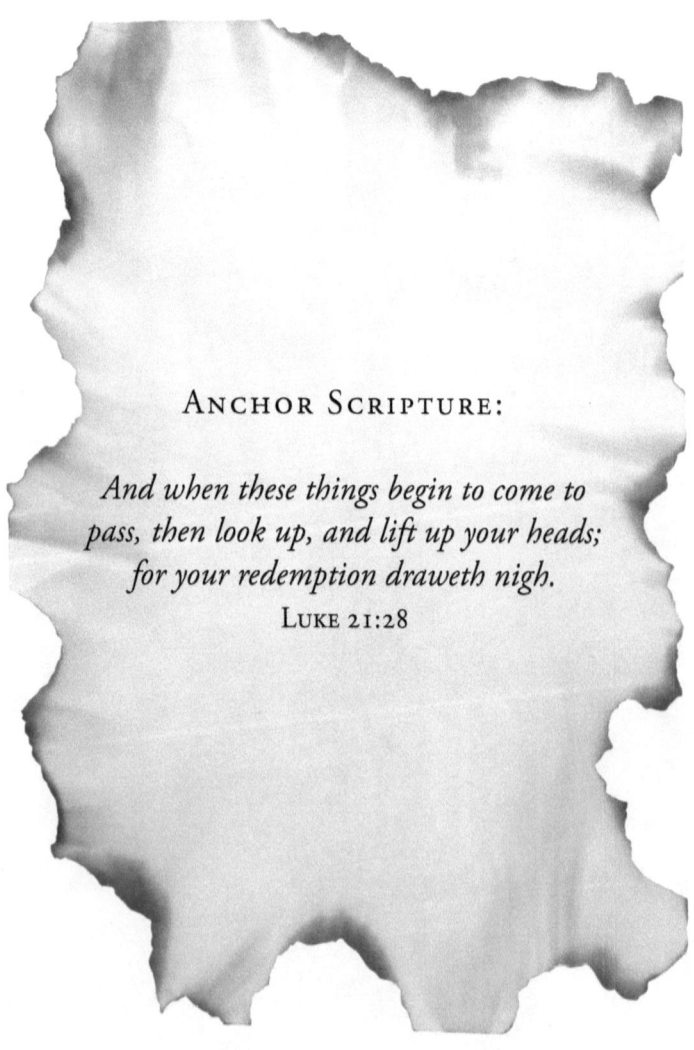

ANCHOR SCRIPTURE:

And when these things begin to come to pass, then look up, and lift up your heads; for your redemption draweth nigh.
LUKE 21:28

EPILOGUE

It is evident that we are living in the final hours of the earth. So many things are happening these days that signifies this earth will no longer be our home. The global holocaust is not a theory or the imagination of man as you may think, but what is about to happen.

This earth is very ripe for harvest, and we are in the final hours of the last days of the end time. Right before our eyes, Bible prophecies are being fulfilled at unimaginable speed while the devil is taking his final onslaught against God's creation, man.

The anchor Scripture says that when we see these things happening, we should understand that the end is near. Anytime you hear about war happening, know that it is near. Anytime you hear about outbreak of diseases and terrible things happening around you or in far countries, instead of wondering why that should be, just know that the end is near. Every event in a day shows that the end is coming. The Bible says that we should look up. When you look down, it means that you don't have hope. But when you look up, it means you are trusting in the One who will soon appear, and so you are not shaken.

> *They looked unto him,*
> *and were lightened: and their*
> *faces were not ashamed.*
> PSALM 34:5

When you look up to God, you will never be ashamed. That is why Jesus said that when you see prophecies fulfilled through the events happening around you, to look up. Don't look down, instead look up to him that has the capacity to help you. Many things are happening these days; there is chaos everywhere, and man is very uncertain about what might happen next. But as a child of God, you have been assured of deliverance. The terrible things that are happening every day should give you joy because your Messiah is coming soon.

I live in New York where life is lived at a very fast pace, and I love to watch the weather news every morning before I leave the house.

The New York weather forecasters are very professional in what they do, and they always predict the weather, and with the information I get from them, I prepare myself for the day. If we could take the Word of God seriously the way I take the weather news, then we all would be safe from the impending holocaust. There is coming a global holocaust and by the help of the Holy Spirit, I have shared with you what you should know, what you should expect and what you should be prepared for, and if this is taken seriously, then you will be saved.

My prayer is that everyone who reads this book will believe it, and prepare themselves to meet with Jesus when He appears, and while waiting, you will be saved from the impending holocaust.

GLOBAL HOLOCAUST

May the Lord bless you and keep you:

May He be gracious unto you,

May the Lord lift up
His countenance upon you

and give you peace
even in such a time as this,

Amen.

VICTOR ANSOR

OTHER BOOKS BY THE AUTHOR

WAR IN THE HEAVENS:
An Exposition Into Strategic Spiritual Warfare

THE SPIRIT OF SERVANTHOOD

HOW TO BE TEN TIMES BETTER THAN YOUR PEERS

If you have been impacted, blessed or given your life to Jesus through reading this book, please don't hesitate to reach out to me through the following medium.

victoransor@gmail.com
Twitter: @victoransor
Facebook: Victor Ansor
Instagram: victor ansor

God Bless You.

Note from the Publisher

Are you a first time author?

Not sure how to proceed to get your book published?
Want to keep all your rights and all your royalties?
Want it to look as good as a Top 10 publisher?
Need help with editing, layout, cover design?
Want it out there selling in 90 days or less?

Visit our website for some exciting new options!

www.chalfant-eckert-publishing.com

www.ingramcontent.com/pod-product-compliance
Lightning Source LLC
Chambersburg PA
CBHW030323080526
44584CB00012B/687